The Power of Appreciation

in Everyday Life

By the same author:

The Power of Appreciation: The Key to a Vibrant Life

The Power of Appreciation in Business: How an Obsession with Value Increases Performance, Productivity & Profits

Winner Takes All: The Eight Keys to Developing a Winner's Attitude

Dangerous Relationships: How to Identify and Respond to the Seven Warning Signs of a Troubled Relationship

Everyday Miracles

The Power of Appreciation

in Everyday Life

Dr. Noelle C. Nelson

INSOMNIAC PRESS

Library and Archives Canada Cataloguing in Publication

Nelson, Noelle C.
   The power of appreciation in everyday life / Noelle C. Nelson.

ISBN 1-897178-22-0

1. Self-actualization (Psychology) 2. Gratitude. I. Title.

BF637.S4N448 2006   158.1   C2006-903895-3

Printed and bound in Canada

Insomniac Press
192 Spadina Avenue, Suite 403
Toronto, Ontario, Canada, M5T 2C2
www.insomniacpress.com

Dedication

This book I dedicate to my clients, readers, workshop participants, and all those I have had the blessing to work with over the years, for it is you who have inspired and motivated me to continue my ardent pursuit of appreciation.

Acknowledgments

Special thanks to Mike O'Connor, my publisher, for seeing the value of this book, and to my editor, Dan Varrette, who tugged, poked, and prodded it into such fine shape. My heartfelt gratitude to Diane Rumbaugh and Michelle Masamitsu, who support all my work in splendid fashion, with patience and unflagging good humor. I offer my profound thanks as always to my family and friends, whose love fills my life with joy.

Thank you!

Table of Contents

The Power of Appreciation with Work and Money

Preface

I wrote *The Power of Appreciation in Everyday Life* as a sequel to *The Power of Appreciation* because I received so many requests for specific ways to apply appreciation to the concerns of our everyday lives.

The Power of Appreciation explains the scientific foundation and principles of appreciation. In a nutshell, appreciation is a scientifically proven energy, much like electricity, that can be harnessed to bring about astonishing benefits to your life in every arena: self, home, love, and work. Appreciation is not a synonym for gratitude; it is actually composed primarily of valuing. Valuing is recognizing and acknowledging that someone or something matters to you, what their worth is to you, what they mean to you—in short, what their value is to you. Gratitude is the emotional secondary (and virtually automatic) component of valuing.

The Power of Appreciation in Everyday Life gives powerful insights, skills, and tools to help you work with principles of appreciation in your day-to-day life. It shows you, through practical examples and vignettes, specifically how to use appreciation successfully, thereby making your life easier, more rewarding, and more satisfying. Because appreciation takes many forms, some of the chapters use the words "appreciation" or "valuing" and some of them do not. The message, however, is always the same: it is through valuing ourselves, others, and our world that we improve our lives.

Each of the topics in *The Power of Appreciation in Everyday Life* addresses a specific challenge within our family, our work, in all types of relationships, and in our self-growth and empowerment. The book provides positive and gratifying solutions to those challenges, helping you deal with the ups and downs of ordinary life, with the frustrations, disappointments, aggravations, missed opportunities, betrayals, and stress of it all.

Best of all, *The Power of Appreciation in Everyday Life* shows you how to appreciate in every aspect of your life so that your life can become the joyous journey it was always meant to be.

Thank you for the opportunity to share once again the wonder of appreciation with you!

Dr. Noelle Nelson

The Power of Appreciation
within Yourself

Engage Your Life Force

Things are going along pretty well at work and at home—no immediate crises or problems, you're just cruising along through your ordinary day-to-day. You think you should be satisfied—after all, isn't this the contented life you've always longed for? And yet, you're antsy, restless. So you shop 'til you drop, adding zeros to your credit-card balance so fast that you make yourself dizzy, or you party your brains out for a couple of days, or you flirt outrageously with that cute young thing who occupies the cubicle next to yours.

The next thing you know, you're struggling to pay off a mass of debt on stuff you don't really want but you're too embarrassed to return, you said some really stupid things to people when you were wasted and now no one will return your calls, and you're up on sexual harassment charges from that cute young thing.

You're in crisis! Suddenly life is incredibly busy,

you're scrambling to get yourself back on an even keel, but when you finally do, guess what? You're antsy, restless. And the whole cycle starts all over again. What's going on? You're beginning to think you're a crisis junkie, yet you're not happy when you're at the bottom trying to find the pieces so you can pick them up. So what gives?

It's simple: you don't know how to engage and channel your life energy. That's all. You are blessed with a wonderful energy, your life force, a basic desire to be and do and have—and you don't know how to capture this energy and use it constructively.

Being antsy or restless is your Inner Self's or your Soul's way of saying to you, "Hey, you're not using your life force appropriately. You're operating at about 10% of what you're capable of, and that's not what life's about." It's as though you owned a Ferrari which you only use as a golf cart—it wouldn't make sense. A sports car is meant to race. A human being is meant to live fully.

Unfortunately, what happens too often is that you grab on to whatever will engage your energy right away, whatever will give you a feeling of being alive at the moment. Shopping, partying, or flirting are all ways—among others—of getting your adrenaline going, ways of engaging your life force. And certainly, they work! For a time, you're neither restless nor antsy. Too often, however, you shop, party, or flirt without thinking, "Is this constructive or destructive?" Since you're not thinking ahead, well, the "ahead" part runs its own course, which more often than not ends up being destructive.

What to do?

1) Recognize your feelings of being antsy or restless for what they really are: an indication that you are operating way below your own level of being alive.

2) Take responsibility for those feelings.

Don't mindlessly shop, party, flirt, or do whatever you ordinarily do to quell the antsy feelings. Say to yourself, "Hey, I'm operating at half power here. I'm unfulfilled because I'm not filling myself up with the 'right' stuff for me."

3) Deliberately choose ways to engage your life force that are constructive as well as satisfying.

For example, get involved in a new hobby; participate in a new sport; challenge yourself at work; read a book you'd never ordinarily read; change your habits; drive a new way to work; make new friends; volunteer your services; write a screenplay. In other words, reach, stretch, and grow yourself! That is the true solution to the "antsy restlessness." Reach, stretch, and grow.

When you're a child, your parents and teachers are there to make sure you do reach, stretch, and grow, but once you're an adult, you become your own parent. It's up to you to challenge yourself—no one else can do it

for you. Use your antsy-restless feelings positively, as a reminder that you're settling to
be less than who you truly are, and have the
fun of becoming the full and vibrant human
being you were always meant to be.

*Next week there can't be any crisis. My schedule is already
full.*

—Henry Kissinger

Procrastinating... Again?!

Why are there some things you just can't seem to get around to? Why does the thought of cleaning out the garage or organizing your paperwork for the accountant send you into full-blown, heel-dug-in procrastination? You're not an idiot, you know these things have to be done. With the garage, for example, you put it off and put it off—always in the name of something else that must get done immediately, such as mowing the lawn (although the grass hasn't grown half an inch since the last time you went over it), pulling the weeds (okay, the one brazen weed bold enough to sprout in your driveway), or spending an hour on the phone with your brother-in-law discussing sports scores.

But your spouse has finally had it, pointing out that garages are for storing cars, not "things." Finally, you're up against the wall. You grit your teeth and push yourself in the direction of the garage, only to get the job barely started, and badly at that. "What is wrong with me?" you groan. This is getting down-right embarrassing. How can you not tackle something as mundane as cleaning out a garage?

There's nothing "wrong" with you, so relax. If you examine your life, you'll notice you only procrastinate with certain things. You resist doing what you don't like to do, which is a huge clue in itself. All you have to do to overcome procrastinating is transform what you don't like into what you do like.

"Impossible!" you say. "I'll never like cleaning out the garage. And I'll certainly never go 'whoopee!' at the thought of dealing with paperwork." Perhaps not, but you can make tasks you don't like more enjoyable.

Here's how:

1) Lighten up.

Quit thinking of the garage cleaning as this huge task requiring Herculean effort, which only makes it seem bigger and more onerous than it really is. Every time you think of it, say to yourself: "Oh yeah, the garage—piece of cake!"

2) Break your task down into bite-size pieces.

Work on one piece at a time, accomplishing your task over the period of one week, spending just a couple of hours on it each time. For example, on the first day, move all the boxes and items out onto one side of the garage so you can actually see everything you need to deal with. On the other side of the garage, designate three areas for separate things: one for "keep," one for "toss," and the other for "charity." On day two, take about a quarter of the pile and sort it into the appropriate categories. Your rule of thumb: if it's not a true family heirloom, and you haven't used it for a year, it gets tossed in the "charity" pile. Make sure you are tossing a lot more than you are keeping.

Continue the same process, handling a quarter of your total pile on each of days three, four, and five. By day six, you should be done sorting. Take the "toss" pile to a dumpster and the "charity" pile to your favorite charity. By day seven, you'll be putting the "keep" pile away and feeling pretty good about yourself!

3) Make the task pleasant.

Take your CD player and a couple of your favorite CDs into the garage the entire time you're working there. Music lightens up just about any task, or listen to a good audio book. Have a big pitcher of your favorite lemonade or soda handy. The happier you make yourself while you're doing something you're not wild about, the easier it becomes.

4) Plan a reward for yourself for when you're done.

Give yourself a treat for having accomplished this unpleasant task. Pat yourself on the back. Ask for congratulation from friends or family.

Whenever you have an unpleasant task that mires you in procrastination, lighten it up. Boogie while you vacuum, watch favorite old movies as you do paperwork, chat with friends on your cordless as you fold the laundry. Life is meant to be an enjoyable experience. Any time you can bring pleasure to a task, you are fulfilling one of life's most important purposes.

The beginning is the most important part of the work.

—Plato

Optimism or Delusion?

You've had a perfectly miserable day at work. Your hours have been cut back. There's no more over-time. The new boss has suddenly decided to give *all* her attention to reorganizing your department (which basically means finding fault with everything you've done), regardless of the fact that you've been doing things for umpteen years exactly the way you were told to by your recently terminated old boss. Then your car broke down on the way home. You spent a miserable two hours waiting for the tow truck. When you finally get through the door and recount your tale of woe to your loving husband, what does he blithely say? "Oh, don't worry, dear, everything will turn out just fine."

You could scream. What the heck does that mean? *"Everything will turn out just fine"*? Everything is awful! Disastrous! Didn't he hear a word you just said? Maybe not. You give your husband the benefit of the doubt. You recount the whole story all over again, he listens sympathetically, then says, "It'll be all right. You just have to be more positive. Everything's going to turn out just fine." Sure, you think. And Santa Claus is real. Off you go to drown your sorrows in whatever's handy.

Well, actually, your husband's words hold a grain of truth. Adopting a positive attitude is indeed the key. Unfortunately, when a positive attitude isn't backed up with a positive approach and an action plan, that key won't open any doors to solutions. This is why "being positive" or "optimism" has acquired such a bad rap. Merely using positive words or having an optimistic vocabulary isn't effective. Transforming a negative situation into a positive one requires a change in approach and action. Everything turns out fine when you have the courage to deliberately go about making it turn out fine. True positivity takes guts.

Where do you start? How do you transform a negative situation into a positive one?

1) Actively look for the possible benefit, the advantage, the gem buried in the negative situation.

Your new boss' laser focus on your department may hurt like heck, but it's also a golden opportunity to get to know your new boss and how she likes things done.

Your car breaking down is an opportunity to review how you maintain your car. Maybe servicing it only when it groans and wheezes isn't the best approach. Maybe being loyal to a service center because you've always gone there isn't advantageous. Maybe this is the perfect opportunity to look into a more customer-focused towing service.

2) Actively follow through with actions and behaviors to get the benefits that exist in the negative situation.

In your work situation, for example, drop your preconceptions about how things "should" be done, quit defending how you did them, and focus on learning your new boss' preferences. Become her most willing student and you will absolutely benefit.

As for your car, schedule regular maintenance visits. Shop around for a service center and/or a towing service that meets your current needs, not those you had fifteen years ago. Use your new-found positive attitude to figure out appropriate approaches and actions that will bring you the positive results you want.

Words alone don't cut it. If you're diagnosed with a dreadful disease, saying, "Well, things always turn out for the best," and leaving it at that isn't optimism; it's delusion. Things turn out for the best when you purposefully look for ways to make them turn out for the best and then pursue those avenues.

Bear in mind that "the best" may be different things to different people. For one person with a dreadful disease, "the best" is seeing an opportunity to totally revamp their habits and lifestyle. For another it may be the opportunity to clean up old emotional business. The particular benefit you find within the negative situation is itself unimportant; it's the ability to find a positive, and to go after it with gusto, that is essential.

The habit of looking on the bright side of every event is worth more than a thousand pounds a year.
—Samuel Johnson

The Sting of Criticism

You dearly love your friend Emmy Lou, but it seems every time you get together, she spends half the time criticizing you, picking at what you're wearing, your latest hairstyle, your Raybans, or your work habits. If it's not one thing, it's another. Then there's your mother-in-law, who is the sweetest lady in the world, yet always has that one little dig she gets in about how your pot roast just doesn't quite make the grade, or how your five-year-old really should be better behaved, or how you look just a little pudgy—have you gained a few pounds? So by the time your husband innocently says, "Gee, honey, shouldn't we get the carpets cleaned?" you either burst into tears and run miserably out of the room, or bite his head off, depending on your style.

Why the overreaction? You're a big girl, you know how to set limits with people. You don't let yourself get trampled on or abused. You're perfectly capable of standing up for yourself, so why aren't you doing that here? Because you've just been busted.

The comments made by your friend, your mother-in-law, and even your husband all zero in on something *you* don't feel comfortable and secure about, an area *you* aren't happy with. You're not secure in your choice of wardrobe. You're not so sure your latest trendy hairstyle fits your not-so-trendy face. Your Raybans have a big old scratch on them. You know you're disorganized at work. The pot roast? You were faking it—you lost the recipe and were winging it. Your five-year-old? You feel distinctly parenting-challenged. And yes, you did gain a few pounds. On top of it all, you know your carpet needs cleaning, you just never seem to have the time to get to it.

Criticism is a funny thing: it only hurts if you're willing to accept it as having some truth. If someone says you're stupid, it hurts, because just about all of us fear that perhaps we aren't as smart as we tend to assume; yet if someone calls you purple in a demeaning tone of voice, it doesn't affect you at all. Why? Because you have no qualms that maybe you really are purple. You don't fear being purple at all.

Does this mean you should sit there and meekly accept whatever criticism someone is willing to dish out? Of course not! Use the criticism constructively to your benefit.

Here's how:

1) Use the criticism as an opportunity to learn more about yourself.

When you feel the sting of a critical

comment, don't defend against it. Instead, ask yourself why that hurt. What are you insecure about here? Figure it out.

2) Make a deliberate choice that resolves your insecurity.

For example, if you're insecure about your parenting skills, choose to improve them. Make a decision to take some classes, read some books, or surf the Internet for help. If you've gained a few pounds, decide whether you are content with your new weight. If you are satisfied, terrific; deliberately choose to be happy in your new expanded birthday suit! If you're not, deliberately choose to explore which weight loss approach will work best for you and go for it.

3) Stand tall and proud with your choice.

When your mother-in-law makes a snide comment about your inability to civilize your child's table manners as your beloved Timmy shoves food in his mouth with both hands, smile with the knowledge of all that you are learning in your parenting class, and say, "Timmy and I are working on his table manners in a way that makes sense to both of us." When your girlfriend remarks about your growing girth, and you've made the decision to love your expanded self, then you can say, "Yes! I am so much more comfortable with a few more pounds on me—I actually enjoy exercising more now that I'm not obsessed with burning off calories."

Criticism is only hurtful if you allow it to be so. Take that sting of criticism and transform it into an opportunity to develop into the wonderfully secure and happy being you were always meant to be.

It is necessary to the happiness of a man that he be mentally faithful to himself.

—Thomas Paine

On Wanting Perfection

Valentine's Day is fast approaching, and this time you've vowed to get it just right. Last year, you were so locked up with work and other stuff that you completely forgot about the whole thing, which led to a perfectly miserable two weeks while your spouse got over it. You've decided to really make it up to them this year. You've made reservations at their favorite restaurant where that band they just love will be playing, saved up to book a limo to take you both there, and bought a new outfit for the occasion. You remembered the card, the gift—everything's going to be perfect.

But then your spouse can't find a thing to wear and is not pleased with having to improvise an outfit at the last minute, and the limo driver can't find your apartment (which is ridiculous, it's not like you're living out in the sticks). By the time the limo gets there, you're already late for your dinner reservation, which doesn't make a darn bit of difference because when you do arrive at the restaurant, guess what? They didn't have your reservation down anyway and they're sold out. Sorry!

In a fit of frustration you wail, "I can't believe this, I just wanted it all to be so perfect!" while your spouse, who after all does see your efforts, tries to console an inconsolable you. What a miserable ending to what was supposed to be your perfect Valentine's evening! And how unnecessary.

Huh? Yes, unnecessary. You fell into the trap of wanting "perfection," which inevitably leads to disaster, rather than aiming for responsibility, which inevitably leads to success.

You see, perfection doesn't exist in the long term. Perfection is something you might achieve in a moment, but it immediately disappears because life is about change, and perfection is static. You can't control life, and perfection requires complete control of all elements. The only things you can completely control are inanimate objects such as fence posts (and even that's open to discussion). Limo drivers, mâitre d's, and your spouse are most definitely not inanimate objects! Responsibility, however, is infinitely adaptable to change, for responsibility is the ability to respond to any given situation at any given point in time.

So when your spouse can't find a thing to wear, help them improvise an outfit, and praise them on their creativity! When the limo driver can't find your place, don't fuss and fume, give him the directions. Keep your spouse entertained by making up silly love poems, or whatever else will keep both of you in a Valentine's mood. When the restaurant can't find your reservation, say, "Wonderful! Darling, what's your heart's desire? I'll take you wherever you want to go!"

In other words, keep responding positively to each and every situation, rather than dwelling on your present misery and staying stuck just because things didn't turn out "perfectly."

Life isn't about perfection. Life is about having a wonderful time enjoying as much of this earthly experience as humanly possible. Whatever happens, remember your ability to respond, and use it enthusiastically. You'll be delighted at just how much fun this very imperfect life can be.

This is the very perfection of a man, to find out his own imperfections.

—St. Augustine

Backside Woes

You're in decent shape. At least you thought you were, until summer hit and putting on your bathing suit woke you up to the horror of your backside. You're appalled. Whatever happened to your well-rounded, nice, tight behind? When did it turn into this lumpy thing that sort of just hangs there? How could this possibly happen?

Yesterday you were 25, and today you're 102—or so it seems from the look of your butt.

Now what? You throw yourself into an exhausting exercise regimen with special "butt blasting" sessions, but after two weeks of dragging yourself home nightly from the gym—sweaty and bone weary, with a barely noticeable "lift" to show for it—you realize that you can't keep going at this pace even if it did eventually work. You can't keep going into work half asleep, and besides, your backside has only minimally improved. You groan. There's no way you can firm that thing up within your prepaid six weeks, if ever. You're getting desperate. You've even considered buying one of those miracle creams they advertise on the TV at two o'clock in the morning—you know, the ones guaranteed to make you look sixteen again with just one application. Uh-huh. You're embarrassed that you even thought of it. But what to do? You're not into plastic surgery, and you don't want to go to the beach in a caftan!

So don't. It's not your rear end that's the problem here. The problem is your wholehearted acceptance of the image of what a backside should look like as perpetuated by the advertising industry. Firm rounded bottoms sell cars, pizza, suntan oil, magazines—and just about everything else. You've confused what is essentially an advertising hook designed to sell products with a beauty standard we're all expected to measure up to. And that's what's got you in such a tizzy—trying to measure up to an unrealistic standard.

Well, the good news is that all behinds are wondrously unique, and all behinds change over time. Some change a lot, some change a little, but all behinds change.

Instead of bucking the current version of your rear end, wear your backside with pride! After all, it performs its primary function—serving as a cushion between your bones and the chair—admirably. Have you ever thought of how many times a day your butt has served you faithfully and well, year in, year out, with hardly a complaint?

Pay attention to the larger issue here. Too often we view our bodies with censure, sometimes for not conforming to whatever the latest fad is, sometimes for showing the wear and tear of the years. In either case, we are also damaging our self-esteem by tacitly assenting to the message that we aren't good enough, that we aren't a worthy member of the human race. Self-esteem, feeling like a person with the right to be here on this planet, is the basis of your ability to be and do things effectively in the world. Eroding your self-esteem for any reason is a dangerous thing to do, for it interferes with your competence in the world and thus with your potential for success and joy.

Don't allow an artificially created standard to mess with your self-esteem! Be appreciative of your body, with all its marvelous parts. Do whatever amount of exercise feels appropriate and good for the whole of your physical well-being, not for the approval of other people.

Be proud of your wondrous behind, whatever it looks like, for you are a fine and glorious human being, here to experience life as it is, not as some advertiser imagines it.

The greatest thing in this world is not so much where we stand as in what direction we are moving.
—Oliver Wendell Holmes

Appreciate Your Way to the Body Beautiful

You pull your pants on and tug mightily at your zipper. Forget it—it's never gonna happen. You groan. Where did those new pounds come from? You were unhappy enough with the shape you were in a few months ago, and here you are, heavier still.

Or, you glance in the mirror before stepping into the shower and freak. How did all that flab get there? When did your butt drop a full three inches? Okay, six inches—and let's not even talk about the underside of your arms. You debate whether to drape a towel over the bathroom mirror or just get rid of the whole thing altogether.

Every time you see yourself in the mirror, you grimace; every time you pull on a pair of too-tight pants, you're disgusted; every time you see a slender toned body on somebody else, you get upset. So you go on a diet (for the umpteenth time) and get yourself to the gym (also for the umpteenth time) but nothing's working. The pounds don't drop off, your body isn't getting any more muscular, you're beside yourself. Why aren't you getting anywhere?

It's because you're giving yourself mixed messages. On the one hand, you tell yourself that your body is gross and disgusting; on the other hand, you go on a diet and exercise, telling yourself you want to be slender and toned. Your subconscious, which listens to *everything* you say, is trying to make both desires come true, and since that is physically impossible, nothing is happening. You're stuck!

How can you get past this conundrum? Give your subconscious consistent messages.

Appreciate the body you have as you look to developing the body you want. "Huh?" you say. "Appreciate the body I have?! How am I supposed to do that? The body I have is the very reason I'm dieting and exercising—I don't appreciate it one bit!" And you're right, it's virtually impossible to look in the mirror at the pudgy mass clinging to your thighs and say, "I appreciate you." It's beyond most of us to value and be grateful for ten pounds of cellulite. Fortunately, you don't have to appreciate cellulite in order to appreciate your thighs.

Switch your focus from what you hate about your thighs to what you *can* appreciate about them. For example, appreciate what willing servants your thighs are. Value how they carry you from place to place any time you want. Be grateful that your thighs don't go on strike periodically and refuse to get you from chair to bed or from up to down. Be grateful that your thighs dutifully provide wonderful support to the upper part of your body. Value how healthy your thighs are, how beautifully the muscles, ligaments, and tendons work together, how little you have to think or worry about them. There is much to appreciate about a thigh, no matter how big or small!

Use this same approach for any body part or your whole body. Value your body's health and strength. Be grateful for how beautifully it functions. Thank your body for giving you energy to go about your day. Be grateful for your body's willingness to sit, stand, eat, read, sing, hike, play—whatever you ask it to do. Get creative. Find as many things to appreciate about your body—warts and all—as you can.

Change what you observe when you look into the mirror. Switch your focus from what you don't like to what you do like—things that have nothing to do with "fat/thin." Value your smile, appreciate the color of your eyes. Appreciate the cut of your hair, how nice your nails look, or how well your accessories coordinate with your outfit. You can find many things about your image to appreciate.

The more you appreciate the body you already have, the more consistent your messages are to your subconscious, and the easier and quicker your path to that slender toned shape you so eagerly desire!

The greatest achievement of the human spirit is to live up to one's opportunities and make the most of one's resources.
    —Luc de Clapiers, marquis de Vauvenargues

New Year's Doldrums

Oh, you did have the very best of intentions. You stood before your mirror on December 28th and solemnly promised yourself: "January 1st (okay, January 2nd), *I will* go on that diet, I will religiously exercise for one hour three times a week, and I will be nicer to the kids." Satisfied, you proudly marched out of the bathroom, and for the next few days you felt oh-so-good about yourself. And when January 2nd rolled around, right on cue you tossed out the still half-full bag of potato chips and ditched the last of the Häagen-Dazs without even a backward glance. You took yourself off to the gym and valiantly huffed and puffed through a full workout. That night, you remained astonishingly pleasant to the kids even as they pouted and whined at bedtime. Very pleased with yourself, you climbed into bed and virtuously told your spouse of your achievements, who snuggled close to you and cooed words of praise. Life was good.

Life, however, was distinctly less good by the end of the week, when you were too stiff to lift a garbage pail, much less a barbell. You thought, "What's the use of going to the gym if I can't work out?" and figured the only way to feel better was to have a cookie. After all, you'd been "good" the whole week, so what's the harm in a cookie? Or two or three, or, what the heck, you've already broken your diet, so you might as well finish the whole box.

And the kids? Well, who can blame you for losing your temper with them when they not only dunked the cat in the toilet but broke the expensive computer toy you'd bought them for the holidays (depriving yourself of that nice sweater in order to do so). And when you said, "Too bad, you aren't getting another one," they wailed that you were so unfair and how much they hated you!

So much for this year's New Year's resolutions. Now you're depressed, miserable, and feeling very bad about yourself. What an unpleasant way to start a year! Yet this is all too familiar a story. Why is that? "What is wrong with me," you ask, "that I can't keep a simple resolution?" You meant well and had such high hopes!

There is nothing wrong with you, your intentions, or your high hopes. Where you faltered is in not recognizing what it takes to change a long-standing habitual behavior.

New Year's resolutions are like quantum leaps. You don't bother making a New Year's resolution unless you're trying to change a behavior that's well entrenched. And in many cases, you want to change it radically. The hope is that with the symbolic fresh start of the New Year, you can make a fresh start with a new habit. Unfortunately, there's nothing fresh or new about *you*. On January 1st (or 2nd), you are still the same person you were December 31st, with the same ingrained ways of thinking about things and doing things. It is unrealistic to expect yourself to be able to function completely differently just because it's a new day.

What's the solution? Never to make a New Year's resolution? Of course not! There's great symbolic value in the beginning of a New Year, and your subconscious will respond to that. Once you make your resolution, however, figure out a series of small steps that will lead you to the goal of your resolution.

For example, instead of going on a radical diet, start gently by replacing sugary deserts with fruit. Don't try to do a full workout three days a week right away; start by getting to the gym once or twice a week and doing a twenty-minute workout, maybe only stretching at first.

Give yourself and the kids some quality time in the evening after they have been fed and bathed and have settled down, when it's easier to be pleasant. Start establishing a more harmonious relationship that way, rather than forcing yourself to be pleasant when the kids are being total brats.

Respect the process of change. Make those New Year's resolutions absolutely, with conviction, enthusiasm, and strong desire, but then plan for the changes you need to make in order to be successful. Oh, and here's the final good news: you can make a

New Year's resolution any time in January (or even February!); after all, it's still a delightfully New Year.

There is no medicine like hope, no incentive so great, and no tonic so powerful as expectation of something better tomorrow.

—Orison Swett Marden

Doomed Resolutions

This year, you swear it's going to be different. This year, you *will* maintain your New Year's resolutions past January 10th, or so you say. Yet here you are, already doubting your ability to stay true to your word. You're appalled. You berate yourself: "I have no character, no spine, no guts! How could I already be reneging on promises I made to myself?" You drag yourself around, feeling horribly guilty, already knowing you won't see your resolutions through much longer. "Might as well give up right away," you sigh.

You declare yourself a loser. The first thing in the New Year? Not a good self-esteem move, and not a necessary one. After all, what were your New Year's resolutions? You were going to quit smoking, spend more time with your kids, be nicer to your ex, and maybe make a real effort to eat healthily. These are fine resolutions! There's no reason why you can't stick with them, you just need to find a way to make them doable.

How do you do that? In 3 easy steps:

1) Prioritize your resolutions.

Don't try to accomplish all of your resolutions at the same time; it'll never work. One of the reasons most people never see their resolutions through is that they try to accomplish all of them at once. You'd have to be a superhero to do that, and even they might have trouble with it.

Instead, prioritize your resolutions, starting with the easiest one. You're not doing any of this to impress anyone, so there's no need to start with the most challenging one. On the contrary, when you start with your easiest resolution, you're more likely to be successful. Success breeds more success.

2) Have a plan.

Let's say you've decided the easiest resolution to accomplish is spending more time with your kids. It's the one that tugs at your heart the most, something that will give both you and your children pleasure. Great! How are you going to do that? Thinking, "Well, I'll just do it," is an admirable sentiment, but not likely to get you anywhere. Instead, make a plan.

Figure out just when you're going to spend more time with the kids and how you're going to make that time available.

Maybe you decide to devote Saturday mornings exclusively to your children. How does that fit with what you currently do on Saturday mornings? If Saturday mornings have been errand-running time, what time do you now set aside for errand running? How about lunch time during the week, or on your way home from work? Then give some thought to what you will do with your kids during your Saturday mornings together. Once you've worked out the "how" and the "what," you'll find it much easier to actually fulfill your resolution.

3) Give yourself support.

You probably don't need much encouragement to spend more time with your children, but you undoubtedly will with other of your resolutions. For example, what about your resolution to stop smoking? That can be daunting in the absence of providing yourself with support. Let's say you're going to use a nicotine patch and gradually decrease the number of cigarettes you smoke—that's your plan.

Give yourself support by enlisting a friend's help so you have someone to check in with or talk to when the going gets rough and you don't want to stick to the plan. Another way to give yourself support is to reward yourself systematically along the way. Give yourself a treat for every week you stick to your plan.

New Year's is a wonderful time to start fresh, a perfect time for resolutions (although really any time of year will do), and now you have a way to make them stick!

Life consists not in holding great cards, but in playing those cards you hold well.

—Josh Billings

Only the Lonely

Here it is, Saturday night, and there you are, eating a TV dinner in front of the tube, getting depressed. You know the pattern all too well. By 9 p.m., you're miserable; by 10 p.m., you're out of control; by 11 p.m., you're picking up somebody completely inappropriate in a bar; and by 2 a.m., you're wondering what to do with this total stranger snoring in your bed. You spend the next month and a half trying to get rid of him.

Your friends *tsk-tsk* and tell you all the things you are doing wrong, which only makes you more miserable, which means that given another month or so, you'll do the same thing all over again. Your life is beginning to resemble a bad soap opera, only this is real life, and it hurts.

What is wrong with you? Why can't you be strong and wait until "Mr. Right" comes along? You are totally disgusted with yourself because it's not like you don't know what you're doing is self-destructive, you just can't seem to stop yourself when you get that lonely.

Let yourself off the hook. It's normal to feel lonely when you're longing for that wonderful relationship you don't yet have. It's totally understandable that you feel miserable when Saturday night hits and you're dateless. Being disgusted with yourself for trying to rid yourself of your loneliness, however, doesn't help. Instead, take positive care of yourself!

Here are some ideas on how to do that.

1) Develop a support system you can turn to when the craving to be with someone gets too strong to resist.

Enlist the help of some of your single friends. Make an agreement that whenever one of you gets the urge to go do something wildly inappropriate out of loneliness, you'll call one of the others for comfort and general handholding. Know that you're in this together, and be strong for one another.

2) Don't leave yourself without something interesting and fun to do on the weekends.

Plan your weekends ahead of time. Plan Saturday nights with friends, married or single. Fill your weekends with interesting activities: join a book club, take weekend classes, find someone to go hiking or bird-watching with. There are wonderful groups like Sierra Singles, various Marathon (walking and running) preparation groups, and others which don't cost a fortune and can fill your weekends with good people and pleasurable activities.

3) Consider getting a pet.

Dogs, cats, and even birds make great pals. Animals are a terrific source of companionship and are wonderfully positive beings to have around. A furry or feathered friend can help comfort you when the nights feel too long and too lonely.

Loneliness is not an affliction. Loneliness just lets you know that you need other people in your life. There's nothing wrong with that. Do what it takes to be with and around other people, and you'll not only be much less lonely (which greatly diminishes the number of inappropriate people in your life) but you'll also make it that much easier to find or be found by "Mr. Right."

The door to happiness opens outward.
— Søren Kierkegaard

Why Is Everyone Picking on Me?

Things are going along okay at work: you're doing what needs to be done, you think everything is hunky-dory, and then your supervisor says, "Haven't you finished that project yet? You should have started on the next one by now," and you're instantly plunged into a horrible predicament. You're so distressed by her comment, you don't even think to say, "I was asked to take over another part of the project, that's why it's taking longer." Instead, you go straight to "I'm inept, I'm incompetent, I'm going to be fired," and it's all you can do not to burst into tears right there in front of her. You feel so bad that by the next day, you're frightfully depressed, can't get yourself out of bed, and have to call in sick.

Fast forward a couple of weeks... you've been dating a guy for a month or so. You really like him, and you think he really likes you. But then he doesn't call when he said he would and you go into frantic mode. What did you do wrong now? Did you say something he didn't like? Did you do something awful without realizing it? You rack your brains trying to figure it out. You leave him cutesy messages, apologetic messages, guilt-ridden messages (being sure that you're doing the wrong thing all along), and when he finally does call, it's to tell you he doesn't think you have all that much in common, you're a great gal, goodbye. And back you go into the land of the woefully depressed, beating yourself up with: "I did something terrible to turn him off. I'm a worthless human being. I'll never be in a relationship."

What is wrong with you? Why is nothing you ever do good enough? Why is everybody picking on you?

They're not. You are. You're picking on yourself. Instead of standing back and objectively looking at the situation, any time anyone says something to you, you interpret it as blame, as proof that you're unworthy. Instead, see their comments as an expression of what is going on with *them*.

Your supervisor has to keep the work flowing according to deadlines she must meet. She's concerned about *her* deadlines, and either didn't know or forgot that you were given an extra piece of work to do. Your boyfriend is seeking a relationship that meets *his* needs, and he's being honest about that. You're the one who is interpreting these comments as meaning you are a failure as a human being.

What's the solution? To love yourself. "Agghhh!" you cry, tearing out your hair. How can you love yourself when you feel so awful about yourself? Besides, saying that you love yourself is trite beyond belief.

Although it may seem trite, loving yourself in this context means to switch your focus from what's wrong with you to what's right. There are some things you know that are right with you, such as the fact that you are a nice person, that you are considerate, that you care about other people, and so on.

Spend some time every day valuing yourself, your qualities, talents, and skills. Write these down. Make yourself come up with just one new thing every day that you can value about yourself. Over time, you'll find that you are increasingly able to see people's comments as coming from their point of view, and not as a direct attack on yourself.

Eventually, you'll be secure enough with your own value that you'll be able to deal with life's bumps and hurdles objectively, without tumbling into those miserable pits of despair.

You future depends on many things, but mostly on you.
—Frank Tyger

Misery Loves Company

You were terminated from your job. Oh, how you hate that word—*terminated*! Why don't they call it like it is: you were fired! And unjustly, too, for no good reason (other than the boss wanted a job for his new love interest), with virtually no warning. You who gave ten good years to the company! You of all people. You are outraged, miserable, and only too willing to tell the tale to anyone who will listen—and to some who have now heard it one hundred times.

And... your boyfriend left you. Okay, so everybody's had a boyfriend leave them at some time, but this jerk left you for another woman, *after* he'd borrowed $1,000 from you, which he clearly has no intention of repaying! Like you can afford to be out $1,000, especially now that you're out of a job. So, added to your original rendition of "look what my horrible boss did to me" is a refrain of "how could he take the money, dump me, and run?!" both of which you not only repeat to all who will (even superficially) listen but also loop in your own mind endlessly, day in and day out.

You're right. You are in a miserable situation, and it's only natural to cry out in woe. It feels good to point to your wounds, say, "See, I'm hurt!" and have others agree. The problem isn't your wanting your distress acknowledged. The problem is revisiting morning, noon, and night what caused you grief, in addition to who, why, and just how they did it. Justifying your misery over and over again has only one result: keeping you miserable.

Like attracts like. Feeling miserable attracts more to feel miserable about. The less you are willing to lift your thoughts out of how bad "they" made you feel, the less you are able to see what might contribute to your feeling good in the here and now.

This does not mean that you should deny your misery. On the contrary, allow yourself to feel it and feel it fully, but then lay it aside. One of the easiest ways to do that is to take an hour or two to write out all the ways in which you were wronged, the "why," "how," "who," and "what" of it. Once you're satisfied you have it all down on paper, set both the paper and your experience aside, not to forget about it or to pretend "everything's okay now," but in order to move on to healing yourself and the situation. You can't heal while you're focused on the misery—it's like constantly picking at a scab: the darn thing takes forever to heal!

Make a list of all the things you can do, people you can reach out to, or resources you can access in order to remedy the situation. Being proactive puts you back in charge of your life. Taking charge of your life is a great way to feel better about yourself and your situation.

List three or four goals that represent different approaches to your situation. For example, you feel you were fired unfairly. Your list might include: "find a lawyer"; "speak to my union rep"; "take an assertiveness class"; "ask Aunt Helen how she got through her termination"; "look up wrongful terminations on the Web"; and so forth.

You feel that your boyfriend took horrible advantage of you and then walked out on you. Your list might include: "find a support group"; "read up on disastrous relationships and how to spot them"; "learn to protect myself better financially"; "speak to my pastor"; "attend some personal-growth seminars."

Licking your wounds may feel great in the short term, but finding a way to heal them feels great in the long term.

Our greatest glory is not in never falling, but in rising every time we fall.

—Confucius

Who, me? Stressed?

You love your family dearly, but right now they are driving you positively buggy. You're waging the battle of the belly-button/nose/tongue piercings with your teenage daughter, your husband is jammed with deadlines at work and can't help out with chores, and your five-year-old has a persistent case of the unanswerable "why, Mommy?"

As if that weren't enough, your supervisor has blithely dumped your vacationing co-worker's tasks in your lap. But mercifully, it's Saturday, the kids are at their respective Saturday activities, your husband is at work, and you've done your chores (enough, anyway) and are off to spend a couple of quiet, blissful hours communing with nature.

Then it starts. The sneezing. The tickle in the throat. More sneezing. You're thinking, "What is this? I feel fine!" You ignore it. More sneezing, tickling, sneezing, until finally, in complete disgust, you throw down your garden tools and yell, "Great! I finally get a little time to myself to putter and now I have *allergies*?!" You've never had allergies before. You're frustrated and aggravated. What is going on here?

Stress. Allergies, headaches, stomach pains and other symptoms are often directly related to your stress levels.[1] As your stress level increases, your body frequently responds by developing various physical symptoms. How you think and feel directly affects your physical state. As Dr. Candace Pert notes: "Your brain is extremely well integrated with the rest of your body at a molecular level [...] We can no longer think of the emotions as having less validity than physical, material substance, but instead must see them as cellular signals that are involved in the process of translating information into physical reality, literally transforming mind into matter."[2] When you're stressed, your body feels it, and your physical well-being suffers proportionately.

You know that your teenage daughter won't turn into the poster child for "Mom knows best" overnight; that your husband's deadlines won't disappear; and that whenever your co-worker returns, something else is sure come up at work. Yet reducing your stress levels isn't about being problem free. Reducing your stress levels is about changing how you think and feel about what is going on. A great way to do that is to appreciate.

Appreciation is one of the best stress-reducers around. Appreciation lowers blood pressure, evens out heart rates, and dramatically improves the functioning of your immune system. Appreciation

1 Information in this chapter should not be used to diagnose or treat a health problem or disease. Please consult a licensed health care provider regarding any medical condition.

2 Pert, Candace B., *Molecules of Emotion*. New York: Simon & Schuster, 1997, 135.

increases blood flow to your brain so that you think better, making you a better problem solver, which in turn lowers stress.

Appreciating isn't hard to do as long as you remember you're not trying to appreciate the troubles in your life, you're simply choosing to spend some time focusing on what *is* working.

Your teenage daughter might be annoying, but she's a healthy, energetic kid, raring to explore the world around her. This you can appreciate.

Your husband isn't available to help out right now, but he is dedicated, working hard to contribute to the family's welfare.

Your five-year-old will outgrow the "Why, Mommy?" stage eventually, and in the meantime, you can appreciate his wonderful desire to learn.

You may resent the extra workload that your supervisor assigned you, but you can appreciate her confidence in your ability to do so and the chance to push your own envelope.

The more you appreciate, the more you'll see just how much appreciation can reduce stress and contribute to your physical, emotional, and mental well-being.

A cloudy day is no match for a sunny disposition.
—William Arthur Ward

Walk off Your Stress

You're upset. You had another fight with your spouse, and even though the fight wasn't a bad one, it was a fight. Worse than that, it was a completely unnecessary fight. Your spouse told you that you're angry at everything, that if the slightest thing doesn't go according to plan, you blow up.

You hate to admit it, but they're right. You're yelling too much. You're yelling at the kids, you're yelling at the dog, you're yelling at car alarms going off. It's not good. You try to tell yourself you're just going through a stressful period and you should chill, but that sage advice only lasts until the next thing sets you off and you're yelling again.

You see ads on TV that frighten you half to death. Are you one of those chemically imbalanced individuals who needs drugs to keep yourself under control? You read about people who undergo radical personality changes because of brain tumors and run to your doctor, who examines you with great concern, and then turns to you saying, "Physically you're just fine, you just seem a bit wired." You are not reassured. You worry that maybe you have an "anger management" problem. The only thing is, you've never been an angry person, and you don't really feel all that angry.

Maybe what's going on with you isn't about anger. Maybe what's going on with you has to do with *stress*.

Everybody reacts to stress differently. No matter how you react, the bottom line is that when you're under a lot of stress, little annoyances get to you more than they would otherwise. It's like the old "straw that broke the camel's back"—you can only take so much, and then your ability to stay calm and collected disappears. You come apart at the seams. Some people feel worn out by stress: it fatigues them and they become exhausted. Other people feel emotionally "attacked" by stress: they find themselves crying at odd moments or feeling anxious and panicked. Others find their ordinary ability to stay on an even keel disappears: they blow up at things that they would usually just shrug off.

When that happens, take a walk—literally. When you're under a lot of stress and feel like you've just about had it, take a brisk walk for about twenty minutes. Deliberately focus on your muscles, on your breathing, and on relaxing as you walk. Think of yourself as "walking out" your stress. You'll start a whole chemical chain reaction in your body that will calm your mind and make it easier for you to weather this stressful period without blowing up.

You can use walking to ease your stress in two very different ways:

1) Walk off your stress daily.

Go for a walk at lunch time, for example, to walk off the stress of the morning. Take another walk before dinner to get rid of the afternoon's accumulated stress and to allow yourself to have a peaceful evening. You'll find that you sleep much better when you've dissipated your stress in this way.

2) Walk off your stress any time you feel yourself about to blow up, cry, or otherwise come apart at the seams.

Even if you only have a few minutes, taking a short walk with the deliberate intention to release tension will do wonders for your health and well-being.

Write on your heart that every day is the best day of the year.

—Ralph Waldo Emerson

The Hero Within *

There has been much talk about heroes lately. Starting with 9/11, we have seen the very best in ourselves across the globe as we responded to the tragic events. From rescue workers on the scene, to New Yorkers donating time, money, food, and clothes; from people across the nation giving blood, to Canadians rushing to offer stranded American travellers food and lodgings (in many cases their own homes and beds!); from people of every country offering aid of all kinds, to celebrities hosting telethons and kids selling lemonade—the list of those who gave and continue to give goes on and on. We can stand tall, we can stand proud, for we are amazing. We have shown a depth of caring, compassion, and courage that has surprised even ourselves.

We are heroes. It embarrasses most of us even to think that, but it's true. Our capacity to care, our courage, and our compassion didn't just arise spontaneously on September 11. It's not something you

* Written in response to the events of September 11, 2001.

"catch," like a virus; it's something that exists deep within you as an untapped potential from the day you are born: it is your personal Hero Within.

September 11 may be behind us, but its aftermath and ensuing acts of terrorism have made us acutely aware of the fragility and preciousness of human life. The Hero has sprung forth from within each of us, strong, valiant, and true. Have you noticed how much nicer people are to each other since 9/11? Have you noticed how patient we are with one another, how much more thoughtful and considerate? People seem to matter more. When someone asks, "How are you?" it seems as if they really want to know. When you ask for directions, people take care to ensure you understand. More people are slowing down at school crossings and at crosswalks, making sure pedestrians are safely on the other side. There's less honking and fewer rude gestures as people drive the freeways. We seem to have developed greater consideration for one another, a readiness to look beyond our usual preoccupation with ourselves to the interests of others.

Some of this may wear off as crises recede, as the threat of imminent terror diminishes, but that's not what is important. What matters, what is meaningful, is that we have discovered our Hero Within, and we can choose to call on that Hero in our day-to-day lives; we can choose to care more about each other as a matter of course; we can choose to be compassionate rather than impatient, intolerant, or annoyed; we can choose to be courageous, and open our hearts to each other, working through our differences and disagreements rather than using them as weapons against one another.

Beyond that, we can become more caring and compassionate with ourselves. We can choose to be patient with ourselves, instead of browbeating ourselves when we don't get something right the first time; we can be compassionate towards our failings and foibles without stepping into self-pity, loving ourselves genuinely because we are worth loving; we can have the courage to stand up for ourselves with civility and respect; we can be Heroes to ourselves in our own lives.

If we can do this, if we can acknowledge and cherish the Hero we all have within, then we will have gained a treasure beyond compare in the midst of this horror. If we can acknowledge and cherish the Hero within each other, recognizing the enormous depth of caring, compassion, and courage that lies within every human being, we will have come a long way towards what really leads to peace on earth.

Crises refine life. In them you discover what you are.
—Allan K. Chalmers

Danger Lurks

You watch the evening news, thinking, "How could things have gotten this bad?" The world seems to be going to hell in a hand basket. Another drive-by shooting, right on the heels of a bank robbery, and a woman raped in a mall parking lot in broad daylight. You shudder and flip to your favorite talk show—only to watch as the host asks, "How safe are you really?" and, "If you're the victim of a crime, do you know what to do while it's happening?"

That's it. You shut everything off, check and recheck all the doors and windows, make sure the kids are okay, crawl into bed, wrap yourself tightly in the covers—and lie staring at the ceiling for the next two hours, worrying about whether you should have gotten that security system they were advertising for $29.95 a month. Of course, how could such a security system stop anybody? Those burglars and murderers can practically walk through walls. Did you check the back door...? And on it goes until you finally fall asleep, somewhere around 4 a.m., only to wake up yawning and groaning at 6:30 a.m. to a newspaper that heralds in your tranquil morning with stories of violence, crime, and disasters that have managed to crop up in the past several hours.

So you check and recheck all your doors and windows as you leave for the day, admonish your children not to speak to strangers or go off somewhere without an adult, and to pay attention if any kid looks suspicious at school. The list of warnings is so long, you're dropping the kids off before you're done reciting it, but that's okay because they know it by heart anyway.

On your way to work, you make sure the windows are rolled up, that your doors are locked, and that you don't make eye contact with anybody (in case they take offense and pull a gun on you). You let that jackass cut in front of you without showing any sign of being upset (same reason). You circle the parking lot at work five times until you find a spot close enough to the entrance and under a lamp post so you won't be in the dark when you get into your car at the end of day. You smile at the guard, flashing your pass as you walk by. By the time you go through the security entrance, let security inspect your briefcase, use your passkey to let you onto your floor, and fire up your computer (inputting your encrypted code word so you can begin work), you wonder why you are exhausted, anxiety-ridden, and cranky when absolutely nothing is going on to make you so.

Oh, but it is! You are feeling the effects of the chronic "danger lurks" mentality that infests our media and is ever-present in our society. In our attempts to keep ourselves safe from the very real violence that can and does occasionally erupt in our lives, we have put in place an ever increasing number of protective devices, systems, and warnings. The problem is not those devices or systems, the problem is the *attention* you are giving them. Living with the constant awareness of danger puts your body and mind in a state of constant readiness, which is not how you were meant to live. Your emotional, mental, and physical emergency response systems were designed to turn on during brief, intense moments and to turn off during long periods of non-emergency living. Staying on "emergency mode" 24/7/365 leads to irritability, paranoia, fearfulness, anxiety, insomnia, ulcers, exhaustion, anger, and a host of other highly unpleasant symptoms.

What to do? You can't very well single-handedly eradicate all the violence in the world, and just turning off the TV won't do it either. But you can take three very valuable steps to help you greatly reduce your anxiety.

> 1) Switch your focus from one of "looking for the danger" to one of "appreciating the safety measures"; from "There's so much to be afraid of" to "I'm so glad I have doors and locks to protect me. I so appreciate this security guard looking after my safety."

2) With your children, switch from "Don't talk to strangers" (once you're sure they've understood that) and "Watch out for the creepy kids" to "Talk only to people you know" and "Stick with kids who play nice and are happy."

3) Recognize that security precautions exist to protect us from the extremely small percentage of violent and dangerous people. TV and the media incorrectly make this small percentage appear representative of the majority of the population. Reassure yourself that the likelihood of you personally ever being involved in such insanity is infinitesimal and that the protective measures are actually very well designed.

Violence exists, but you don't have to let the fear of it ruin your life. You deserve better!

Men are not prisoners of fate, but only prisoners of their own minds.

—Franklin D. Roosevelt

Fear Paralyzes

As we approach Thanksgiving and are blessedly grateful for so much, it may be challenging to celebrate our thanks with the enthusiasm we had before terrorism entered our lives. Fear dampens your mood. It's it hard to look at your family without immediately thinking of how to protect them, or worrying that you can't. It seems that every day there are new reasons to be afraid: terrorism and foreign wars just don't seem to go away.

A fear isn't so bad when you can stare it in the face and deal with it head on. A hurricane is coming, you batten down. You're diagnosed with cancer, you fight the good fight. But the fears we are subject to on a regular basis since September 11th and the war in Iraq aren't the kind you can stare in the face. These fears are riddled with too many questions: what's going to happen? Airborne toxins released in malls? Deadly bacteria in our water system? Killer viruses affecting everybody? Bombings? Of what kind?

Where's the threat going to come from? And when?

Staying on alert for danger—being in a state of constant fear—is a killer. The terrorists are counting on that, because terrorists don't have what it takes to outfight us in the open. Terrorists wage an underground war, as much on our psyches and emotions as on our bodies. They figure that instilling fear in our hearts will do their work for them—and they are right. If we let them.

Fear paralyzes. Fear stops your thinking at a time when you need it most. Fear weakens you and renders you powerless. That's precisely what terrorists expect us to do: be paralyzed, stop thinking, become powerless.

Terrorists would have us fear life itself, fear the daily doings of life. Like the Afghani women who live behind veils, not allowed to work, learn, or do so many of the ordinary things we take for granted, terrorists would have us live fearful, muted lives, forbidding ourselves to do and go and be as we please.

Defy the terrorists. Refuse to live up to their expectations. Break through the paralysis. Take charge by making yourself ready for whatever comes, whenever it comes.

Get strong.

1) Build your immune system. It is still your single greatest defense against most physical threats. It is your greatest ally in healing.

2) Build your character. Be more courageous,

upstanding, honest, persevering in your everyday life. Develop your wisdom and sense of perspective.

3) Build your caring and compassion. Extend a hand without being asked. Listen without needing to be heard. Seek to understand rather than focusing on being understood. Ease up on your cynicism and impatience, with yourself as well as with others.

4) Build your commitment to yourself, your friends, your family. Make time to connect with nature, with your spirituality. Tend to the love in your life—nurture it, appreciate it. Hug your children more often. Give compliments freely. Pet your dog, your cat, a lot and often.

5) Build your love of life. Live your life with as much gusto as you can muster. Savor every moment of every day. Taste your food more, smell the air around you, notice the trees and clouds. Sing, dance, ride your bike, or squish your feet in the earth. Feel the energy in your body, praise the goodness in your life.

6) Build your faith in a bright and shining future. Set goals for yourself. Keep dreaming your dreams, reaching for that success, that relationship, that happiness. Encourage your children to look forward to "what I want to

be when I grow up" without restriction. Tell tales of pioneers and others who have weathered phenomenal challenges and thrived.

Refuse to let fear rule you. Let this Thanksgiving be an even grander celebration than usual. Get strong and together we will show those who would destroy our world and all that is good in it that they cannot.

Destiny is not a matter of chance, it is a matter of choice; it is not a thing to be waited for, it is a thing to be achieved.
—William Jennings Bryan

Keeping Your Spirits Up

The world is in such a state of constant upheaval: the media keeps us on "violence alert" twenty-four hours a day, the stock market creaks along way below our expectations, companies continue to downsize, and for every kidnapped child who is (blessedly!) found, a handful more disappear.

Fear is omnipresent, whether it's on a global level as threats of international violence hit the airwaves, a national level when the economic news is rife with downsizings and fraud alerts, or a personal level when you discover paroled child molesters are living in your neighborhood, where your three children are still in elementary school.

The stress of all this is a killer. Literally. When you maintain high levels of negative emotion for long periods of time, your body is functioning in emergency mode far longer than it was designed to, and the toll on your body, mind, and spirit is cumulative and great. Your heart rhythms tend to be chaotic, your immune system becomes supressed, and even your brain doesn't function with the same clarity as when you're feeling positive and happy.

But what can you do? How can you keep your spirits up when the world around you seems to be in such dire straits? How can you feel uplifted when there's nothing to be uplifted about?

1) Go back to the basics.
Appreciate the simple things, such as the fact that the world is still turning on its axis, that the sun rises and sets every day, that cats purr, dogs bark, and children play.

Look at your life. Give attention to whatever pleases you in your life, no matter how small it may be: the pleasure of your morning cup of coffee, the smile of a friend, the good feeling of being productive at work or at home, your child's latest achievement. The more you look for reasons to feel good, the more likely you are to find them.

When you find joy in the ordinary events of everyday life, you balance out some of the stress caused by world or national events. Your shift in focus allows you to relax, and with that relaxation, your body, mind, and soul benefit. Happiness is a great soother.

Do not confuse appreciating what is good and of value in your life with denial. There is no need to say, "Oh, the violence in our world doesn't matter. I'll never get fired.

My children are safe no matter what." That would be foolish. Appreciating what's good in your life allows you to adopt a more realistic view of life, one that takes into account both what stresses you out and what uplifts you and brings you joy.

2) Get a broader perspective.

It's easy to forget the bigger picture when you're intensely involved in what's going on right here, right now. Remind yourself that humanity has experienced periods of great violence and destruction, yet humanity has survived. Remind yourself that in the midst of economic disaster, people have found a way to go on. Remind yourself that you have managed to carve out a life which is for the most part good, even when you've had times of great difficulty.

Seek inspiration from the stories of people who have survived and thrived despite seemingly impossible odds. Learn what has helped them rise above desperate situations and think about how you can apply this to your own situation. You don't have to reinvent the wheel!

Many people have been through all sorts of turmoil, have come up with creative and positive ways to see themselves through, and have written or spoken about their experiences. You can benefit from their examples and raise your spirits to that happier, less fearful, healthier level you deserve.

Man never made any material as resistant as the human spirit.

—Bern Williams

The Power of Appreciation
within Your Relationships

Getting to Know You

Your last relationship was a bummer, mostly because you failed to get to know your drop-dead-gorgeous ultra-cool boyfriend before hooking up with him, and as a result found yourself miserably in love with someone who couldn't possibly love you back. You vowed you would never let this happen again. Your new boyfriend? Hey, you know this man almost better than you know yourself. You know his favorite color, his shoe size, what time he gets up in the morning, how he likes his coffee, his mother's maiden name, when he last voted, and what he ate last Thanksgiving. You know which side he likes to sleep on, that he's worried about premature hair loss, that he hates his boss but loves his job, and that he had a mad crush on his first grade teacher.

The problem is, you haven't collected all this information in order to better love your boyfriend, to give him a sense of safety in being known and understood. Nor have you catalogued his preferences, habits, and hobbies to figure out if this person is a suitable match for you. No, you've committed to memory your boyfriend's every like and dislike the better to manipulate him into staying with you, being nice to you, and being impressed by you.

Put this way, it sounds so ugly! Yet we've all been guilty of this to varying degrees. You know he likes mashed potatoes, so you feed him mashed potatoes; you know he likes to go to car races, so you turn yourself into a car race junkie. The problem is not what you're doing, it's the *intent* with which you're doing it.

If you're feeding him mashed potatoes or going to car races to support and validate your boyfriend for who he is, that's terrific. But if you're catering to him in these ways in order to bind him more tightly to you, to make him be nice to you, you're in trouble, because when he doesn't pay more attention to you despite these efforts, when he flirts with a non-mashed potato, non-race car type, you're furious! You feel betrayed. You're indignant and self-right-eous. "After all I do for you!" you fling at him in a voice which can be heard clearly three blocks away.

True love cannot be had through manipulation. A person you get to know so you can wrap them around your little finger may be yours for awhile, but it won't last. Oh, there are exceptions, there are people who crave dependent relationships and some are only too happy to oblige with whips and chains, emotional or otherwise; but these are not tales of true love. These are sad tales of people taking advantage of others' vulnerabilities that often end up as lurid fodder for the tabloids. When you use whatever you've learned about your loved one against him, all you succeed in doing is damaging the relationship. How can someone possibly feel safe and secure (the very foundation of love) when who they are is being used against them? How can anyone feel understood when what is known about them is used to manipulate them?

What to do?

1) Have a loving intent.

There are at least three legitimate purposes for getting to know someone:

To give your loved one a sense of safety in being known and understood;

To determine the suitability of this person as someone you can love and be loved by;

To be able to give to, care for, and respect the person in a way that is meaningful to them.

2) Be honest with yourself.

If you find that you are getting to know someone to manipulate him into being close with you, admit it to yourself. If you're stockpiling ammunition with which to control your loved one, you're not creating a loving relationship. This holds true whether you're dealing with a potential mate, a friend, or your sister.

3) Check in with yourself from time to time.

Ask yourself: "Why do I want to know this? What do I intend to do with this information?" Work with yourself so the answer is more and more often: "Because I want to give him a feeling of being known and understood," or, "Because I want to appreciate, support, and care about them better."

These are the answers of love, and these are the answers worthy of you as a truly loving person.

To love is to place our happiness in the happiness of another.
—Gottfried Wilhelm Leibniz

Oh, the Power of Words!

You step up to the ticket counter at the movie theater and say, "One, please," take your single ticket, and sit your single self down in the darkened theater. You munch from your single-sized bucket of popcorn, sighing as you can't help but notice all the loving couples all around you, cooing and holding hands. Heck, even the ones who are bickering look happy to you! You pop a single piece of popcorn into your mouth and sigh your way through yet another movie where somebody else got the guy... not you... never you... sigh...

"Why are all the good ones taken?" you cry to your equally morose single girlfriends. "Why are men so commitment-phobic?" "Why do men only want one thing, and when they've had it, they're gone?" Your girlfriends agree, nodding sagely, "That's just the way men are." You don't understand why you can't find a relationship, why you're still alone. And in the dead of night that awful little voice starts in: "What's wrong with me? Why won't anybody love me?"

Oh, the power of words! Words are a direct reflection of your thoughts. Your thoughts are what determine what you will perceive, what—out of everything going on around you—you will pay attention to. When you find yourself saying, "All the good ones are taken," you are actually saying, "I won't pay any attention to the good ones who are *not* taken. All I will see as I go about my day are the good ones who *are* taken."

When you say, "men are commitment-phobic," you only notice those who are. You don't even see the men ready, willing, and able to commit, or you never consider them seriously. You find flaws in such men, which is really just a self-fulfilling prophecy, your subconscious way of helping you stay true to your credo: "men are commitment-phobic!" You are inevitably, irresistibly, attracted to those men who are hunters, not gatherers, your subconscious supporting your belief that "men only want one thing." And then you're all upset when you can't find "a good one," and you torment yourself with doubts about your worthiness, your loveability.

Put an end to the self-torture! Put the responsibility for the situation squarely where it belongs: on your thoughts, your beliefs about men—not on your self-worth. Your thoughts are what is creating this unwanted situation. Change your thoughts and you will change your experience of life.

Simply put, your thoughts are not facts. Your thoughts are your version of the facts, and frankly, there are as many versions of the facts as there are people on the planet! That's why when there are six eyewitnesses to a crime, there are six different versions of what happened. Everyone perceives the facts differently. So you might as well let go of the thoughts that don't serve you, that don't match up with what you want, and adopt a new version of the facts that do!

"Men are great," "Lots of men value relationships," "There's a new single one born every minute," "Lots of men are looking for a gal just like me," "Lots of men thrive on commitment." All of these are far more supportive of your desire for a relationship than the thoughts that you usually trot around your brain. These thoughts are every bit as legitimate a version of the facts as your previous thoughts. Nothing stands in the way of your adopting them.

So go for it! Every time you catch yourself having a thought that doesn't support what you want, change the thought. Eventually, you'll start to see men who fit your new thoughts as your subconscious falls into line and allows you to perceive them differently.

Life is a whole lot more fun when you get what you want. You know, two tickets, two seats, and that giant bucket of popcorn!

The universe is change; our life is what our thoughts make it.

—Marcus Aurelius

The Game

You're busily vacuuming the house, determined to get your chores done this morning so you can enjoy a restful Sunday afternoon. You smile as you hear the sound of water running in the kitchen: your husband doing his end of the chores, kitchen clean-up. You work your way down the stairs into the front hall, and frown. Why is the TV on? The kids are at soccer practice; one of them must have left it on this morning. You turn off the vacuum, go into the living room, and stop short, for there on the living room couch sits your supposedly kitchen-cleaning husband, the dishrag dangling from his limp fingers, mouth agape, staring at the TV as if some monumental world event were unfolding before his very eyes.

You groan. *The Game*. He's watching *The Game*. It doesn't matter what day, hour, or year, there's always *The Game* that must be watched. You put on your most determined expression, march yourself over to the TV, and shut it off.

"What did you do that for!" your husband exclaims, aghast.

"You said you'd clean the kitchen this morning," you reply righteously.

"And I was, I am—I just stepped in here for a moment," he counters, reaching for the remote.

"Yeah, right," you say, "and you know what's gonna happen? You know who's going to end up cleaning the kitchen? Me! And there goes my Sunday afternoon! Well I'm sick and tired of it. You don't care about me at all; all you care about is your stupid old *Game*!" you cry out, bursting into tears, running off to shut yourself in the bathroom.

Your husband drags himself over to the bathroom and says through the closed door, "You know that's not true. Do we have to have this argument again? I'm just checking the score—I'll get the kitchen done, quit crying for @#$! sake, jeez."

Somewhat mollified, you dry your tears and go back to your vacuuming. But you can hear your husband complaining under his breath, and you know all too well how the afternoon is going to play out. You'll be disconnected from each other, each sitting in your own stew, and miss out on the lovely Sunday you could have enjoyed together. But what to do? You're right, and he's wrong. You'd agreed that the chores would get done and they're not getting done. You can't very well let him get away with that.

Perhaps not, but you can rethink the situation so that you are both right, both happy, and both doing chores. The problem isn't in your husband's watching *The Game*, even though that's where you're fixated. You think, "If *The Game* just disappeared, none of this would happen—we'd both just do our chores and then have an enjoyable afternoon together." All that you consider are ways to get rid of *The Game*, or ways to get your husband to quit watching it. You are severely limiting your problem-solving abilities by restricting yourself to only one possible solution: eliminating *The Game*.

Instead, take the larger view:

1) Challenge yourself to think creatively.

How might *The Game*, you and your husband, and the unfinished chores all exist happily in the same moment? Once you've clearly identified and formulated the challenge before you, you can set about brainstorming creative solutions.

2) Involve your husband in the process.

People are much more liable to actually implement or follow through on decisions when they actively participate in the decision-making process. Ask him, "Honey, how can we get all our chores done Sunday morning, with you being able to watch *The Game* as well?" Both of you write down all the ideas you can come up with to make this happen.

For example, you might write down, *Husband does the vacuuming and all dusting in the living room and related areas while watching*

The Game. And he might write down, *Get small portable TV for kitchen and watch* The Game *while doing kitchen duty*. Figure out between the two of you what is the best way for *both* of you to get what you want.

Getting stuck on "I'm right" and "This is *the* way to do things" doesn't work in a relationship. Instead, take the larger view and work together so life can be the joy it was always meant to be.

The true test of a first-rate mind is the ability to hold two contradictory ideas at the same time.
—F. Scott Fitzgerald

True Giving

You've been reading *Make Your Relationship Better*, that self-help book your husband has left none-too-subtly lying around. It goes on and on about how giving is important to a loving relationship. No problem! You've got this giving thing down pat. You announce to your beloved, "I'll go with you to your hockey game this weekend if you let me go out with the girls Friday night." He returns with, "Sure, I'll stay at home Friday night all by myself, do diaper duty, and otherwise handle the kids if you let me invite my brother and a couple of buds to come to the game with us." Done deal! It's kind of like an emotional swap meet in your mind—you give a little of this, he gives a little of that, and everything's all well and good. You lean comfortably back into the couch, well pleased with yourself, cross your feet on the coffee table, toss the book aside, and reach for your favorite fashion magazine.

Not so fast there, Ms. Night-on-the-Town.

Contingency giving—giving with an "if"—has its place in a relationship, no doubt. It is, however, giving with strings attached, which most of us remember well from childhood and hated even then. "I'll give you a popsicle if you clean your room before you go out"; "I'll give you the keys to the car if you watch your baby sister this afternoon." Remember your reaction to such giving? "Why can't you just give me the popsicle? Why do I have to clean my room to get it?" "Why can't I just have the keys to the car? Why do I have to baby sit my icky, drooling, baby sister to get them?"

True giving doesn't have any strings attached. True giving is done for the pleasure of doing so, to give pleasure to your loved one, not to get someone to do something. Our parents, however, rarely had the time or energy to say, "You're right. I'll give you the popsicle or the keys to the car for the sheer joy of giving you pleasure, and since you love me truly, you will joyously give me hours of your time cleaning up your room and baby sitting your adorable, still-drooling baby sister without my ever having to suggest these activities, much less having to ask for them." Yeah, right, like that's ever going to work. Raising children may be a labor of love, but it's a highly pragmatic one. You have to teach the kid responsibility and get their help in running this thing called a family, and you don't have all day to do it!

Contingency giving has a place in a loving relationship, but it is not, nor should it be, the only type of giving you do. True giving doesn't expect reciprocity of any kind: it is done purely to give pleasure to your husband. Whether or not you derive enormous satisfaction and pleasure from their happiness is absolutely irrelevant to your giving. Okay, so now you're stumped. You can't just give and give and give. That may work in fairy tales, but come on, this is real life— you have to *get* sometimes, too! Of course you do.

Here's how you deal with it:

1) Respect the different forms of giving.

Sometimes it is expedient to offer something in exchange for something else, and it's important to let your beloved know that. "Honey, you know I don't like going to hockey games, much less with a bunch of guys, and I know you're not crazy about me leaving you alone with the kids on Friday night to go clubbing with the girls, so why don't we make a deal? I go with you to your hockey game with the guys if you'll be okay with me going out with the girls on Friday." Now the deal's above board. There's no manipulation here, the strings are out in the open, and your husband can either accept or reject it.

2) Develop the habit of true giving.

Give from the heart, give for the pure pleasure it brings your husband, without expectation of return, once a day. What do you give? Whatever will bring your husband pleasure. It could be your saying "I love you"; it could be your saying "good morning" with a smile; it could be your making the coffee or tanking up the car; it could be anything at all, from a word of praise to a Rolex watch. It's not the gift that matters, but how it's given.

There is a tremendous joy in true giving. Try it. You'll be amazed at how good it feels—to both of you.

It is not the failure of others to appreciate your abilities that should trouble you, but rather your failure to appreciate theirs.

—Confucius

The "You First" Trap

Your relationship is at a stand-still. Worse than that, it feels like it's in a serious state of decline. You look at your husband, and in the place of that enthusiastic, loving, vibrant man you fell in love with, all you see is an overweight, tired, don't-bother-me guy who says, "Hey, don't look at me, I didn't do it," before you even get to what's on your mind.

Instead of loving your husband, you resent him. You long for the days when he used to listen to you, pay you compliments, bring you the occasional daffodil. Heck, at this point, you'd settle for a grunt, a nod of approval, and a stray weed! You grumble at him, yell, "Why won't you listen to me?!" or storm off and pout, but nothing seems to get through. You make very unsubtle comments about how nice it would be to cuddle while you're watching television, like you used to, and he doesn't even let go of the remote.

You feel unloved, unwanted, unappreciated. Your relationship feels stale, flat, all the love gone out of it.

There is, of course, a very easy remedy for the pathetic shape your relationship is in, and that is to appreciate your husband. To value him for his efforts on behalf of your family, to be grateful for what he does contribute rather than focusing on what he doesn't, to notice and acknowledge all the good he does, which, despite your current frame of mind, is probably considerable.

"Really?" you ask, "*Me* appreciate *him*!?" You purse your lips, batten down your heart's hatches, and barricade yourself behind a wall a mile thick called "you first," as in, "Why do I have to be the one to do the appreciating?" Here you are, feeling utterly unappreciated; it feels completely unfair—not to mention practically unfeasible—for you to "go first"!

You're right. It does feel unfair, no doubt about it. But here's the problem: someone has to break the cycle, someone has to take the first step to shift the unhappy feelings between you and your husband, and you're the one complaining the loudest. If you wait for your husband to take the first step, you may wait a very long time, not because he's a bad person, but because as of right now, he's not the one complaining about it.

So, park your ego and your resentment along with it and get ready for love! Prime that pump by thinking about what specific things you can genuinely appreciate. Figure out whatever it is about your husband that you can sincerely value and be grateful for. Maybe it's that he sticks with a job he doesn't like so he can bring home that paycheck: thank him for his hard work instead of focusing on his complaining. Maybe it's that he does the dishes when you ask him to: thank him for doing them instead of focusing on the fact that you always have to ask (he never volunteers to do the dishes), or that doing dishes should be "normal" and doesn't require any thanks.

The more you find to appreciate about your husband, and the more freely, honestly, and often you tell him of your appreciation, the more likely he is to begin appreciating you. Don't expect him to keep pace with you, though. Just appreciate your husband as a way to prime the love pump, which, if there is any love in your husband for you at all, will help start the flow. Then keep finding reasons to appreciate him, leaving your "you first" objections at the door.

After all, what does it matter who goes first if the end result is a renewed loving relationship full of happiness?

We know the truth, not only by the reason, but by the heart.
—Blaise Pascal

Love Is Not *a Power Struggle*

Your husband grips the remote with a mighty hand, surfing the channels relentlessly for something to pique his interest. You say, "Oh, that looks interesting"; he says, "Boring."

After half a dozen polite attempts, you snap at him: "Well I'm getting dizzy from all the channel surfing. Could you just stick with something for awhile?!"

"Fine," he grumbles, settling on a science channel. You sigh. Oh, great. Another night of watching animals tear each other apart. You huff your displeasure and retreat to the bedroom.

A little later, you hear the refrigerator door close. It's your chance! You race into the living room, locate the remote in record time, and switch to a family-in-crisis movie. Ahhh... Your husband comes back in the room and protests: "Hey, I was watching that animal show!"

"I know," you say smugly, "but now I'm watching this." And the die is cast.

With that, another night of creating distance between you is underway, another night of your love for each other dying just a little bit.

Power struggles do that. Power struggles tear a couple apart. You want the windows open at night, he wants them shut. The battle for power rages as you open them, he shuts them, you open them, he shuts them, all night long. If you can tolerate open confrontation, this battle is waged dramatically, accompanied by yelling and screaming.

If you don't tolerate confrontation, the struggle goes on passive-aggressively: you open the window on your way to the bathroom, he closes it as soon as he thinks you're asleep; you open it when you wake up in the night, he senses your movement, waits again for signs of slumber, then shuts it once more. In either scenario, each of you clings tenaciously to "my way." Getting your way becomes more important than preserving the love between you.

That's the key to resolving the power struggle: recognizing that you are sacrificing your love to your "my way or the highway" mentality. Once you understand the terrible toll that your combined obstinacy is taking on your relationship, you can take steps to do things differently.

You can both be "right." You can both have your individual ways. All it takes is a willingness to value both your husband's preferences *and* your own. When you value your husband's right to his desires, you don't want to squash them either overtly or covertly. When you value your own rights, you're equally unlikely to allow your husband to squash your desires. When you value *both* your own and your husband's desires, you can say, "Your preferences are fine—so are mine! Let's get creative, let's have fun seeing how we can accommodate both of our desires." You are now putting your love first, and asserting your individual preferences in the service of that love. There is no longer a power struggle; there is only a problem to be mutually resolved.

The remote control fight, for example, can be settled by first acknowledging that each of you has different, equally valid preferences. You've just reinforced the love between you. With that emotional support, you can now get practical and figure out the specifics. You may find there are actually only a few shows each of you really care about, and that once the power struggle aspect is gone, figuring out a mutually compatible "TV schedule" is remarkably easy.

Priorities are extremely important in a relationship. When you make your love for each other your first priority, the power tug-of-war loses all appeal.

Hearts are not had as a gift, but hearts are earned.
—W. B. Yeats

Feel the Love

You're caught up in the whirl of your everyday life—your job, the kids, friends, PTA, soccer, cleaning, errands, cooking—the works, and suddenly you remember... Valentine's Day! You rush out to get something to give to your partner and quickly make reservations somewhere, lest you be accused of not loving him. The day comes, you spend a sweet and romantic evening together—and that's that. You zoom off into your hectic life with nary a backward glance.

Or you don't have a partner. You dread Valentine's Day because it only reminds you of the glaring lack of love in your life. You're jealous of people with significant others, those who spend Valentine's Day gazing lovestruck into each other's eyes. You spend Valentine's Day grouchy and depressed.

In either case, you're not feeling the love. All too often, when you are in a relationship, you end up taking the love for granted, and when you're single, you fail to see the love that exists in your life. Either way, you lose out on the enormous power and bone-deep good feeling of love. How does Valentine's Day come into this? Valentine's Day can serve as a powerful reminder to feel the love in your life every day, to value and appreciate it with all your heart and mind so it can feed your body and soul as it is meant to.

When you have a partner, take a moment every day to appreciate them. Perhaps as you take your morning shower, before you start reviewing that list of all you have to do that day, think of how much joy they bring you, how grateful you are for that kind word they said last night, or the way they snuggled against your body this morning. Reflect on the value of their honesty and how much that matters to you, or the music of their laugh and how it uplifts you.

Then, make a point of expressing your appreciation for your partner at least three times that day. It doesn't matter if your way of expressing yourself is an extra long hug as they go out the door, or a note stuck to their coffee mug, or an e-mail sent in the middle of the day; just find a way to express how much you cherish those you love three times a day, every day.

If you are single, take that moment in the shower or over your morning coffee to think of all the love in your life. Perhaps it's your cat's gentle purring as you stroke her fur, or your friend who called to ask how you're doing, your boss congratulating you on a well-done piece of work, or the sun kissing your face. All of these are ways in which those in your life (including nature or God) love you.

Expressing your appreciation for this love in your life at least three times during your day is easy. It doesn't matter if your way of expressing yourself is to call your mom one extra time that week, to spend an extra moment listening supportively to a friend, or to smile gratefully at a co-worker; simply find a way to express your appreciation three times a day, every day.

What you'll find, much to your surprise, is that expressing your appreciation for the love in your life ends up feeling very good—to you. As much as those around you will benefit from your doing so, the one who will benefit the most is you. Your very body benefits from the inner peace and relaxation that expressing appreciation brings with it, and your soul thrives on it.

Make Valentine's Day your every day—and watch your life fill with an abundance of love and good feelings.

Where there is love there is life.
                                        —Mahatma Gandhi

Love to the Highest Power

Valentine's Day is a wonderful day, and you look forward to it. Your husband is a sweetheart and remembers to bring you flowers and candy. You set a nice table, park the kids with your mom, light the candles, and enjoy a romantic dinner together. You talk about how you met, reminisce about your courting days and how you fell in love, and you sigh...

The next morning, you wake up and he's snoring, scruffy-cheeked against the pillow. By the time you've done last night's dishes and made coffee, he's out of the shower, dressed, and completely absorbed in the morning paper. Not a shred of conversation— much less a "thank you" or "Did you sleep well, dear?"—just a quick peck on the cheek as he leaves, *if* you position yourself by the door on his way out.

As you're off to pick up the kids, drop off the kids, and on to work—your regular routine—you wonder, "Is this all there is to love? A commitment to share the load, bring up the kids, and, if we're lucky, get to retirement together? Whatever happened to being in love, to cherishing our mates above all else, to that divine feeling of someone so incredibly special in your life? Is Valentine's Day the only day of the year when we can get even a momentary hit of what that was like?!"

No! You can have Valentine's Day just about every day of the year. You can have that blissful feeling, you can take love to the highest power every day, all it takes is a little appreciation. Appreciation doesn't just mean gratitude; appreciation means to value something *and* be grateful for it. It's something we all do completely naturally and instinctively when we fall in love. You value your husband's smile, his hand holding yours, the way he listens to you, the way he scratches his head when he's thinking. You feel grateful for his very presence in your life, and you tell him of your appreciation over and over.

Unfortunately, over time, our focus shifts. You pay more attention to what you *don't* value about your husband—to his annoying habits, his different ways of doing things—than you do to what you *do* value. And when you don't value something, you aren't grateful for it. You cease to bask in his presence and only feel the love when he's doing something for you that you want or need. You voice your gratitude for those things, but forget to praise him for who he is, or just for his existence in your life.

Make a list of all those things you value about your husband, big and small. Whether it's how he makes the coffee on Sunday mornings, how he carefully tucks the kids in at night, how much he worries about doing the right thing, or how he wants to cheer you up when you're blue—write these things down. Add to the list every day.

Let your husband know, in words, how you value him: "I love how conscientious you are in making decisions, how you want to make sure you take everything into account"; "The way you scratch your head when you're thinking is so cute. It's like you're tickling your brains into action." Be sincere! Be expressive. Take every opportunity to let him know not just that you love him but also why you love him.

Yes, this takes some effort, and yes, you have to go first. And you may find yourself doing "all the valuing, there I go again" for awhile, but it's like watering a plant: the more you value and are grateful for your husband—the more you openly, genuinely, and thoroughly appreciate him—the more the love will grow.

Once you discover the wonder of taking love to its highest power, you can have Valentine's Day every day, not just on February 14th.

Love is, above all, the gift of oneself.

—Jean Anouilh

Saturday Night

It's Saturday night, "date night" in the land of singles. "Date night" in the land of the married or otherwise significantly coupled—you wish! You hear the shower running and your heart lifts. Maybe it will be date night after all. But no, your clean husband bounds into the living room, having made a detour by way of the kitchen, and armed with beer and popcorn plops onto the couch, ready for a few hours of fatiguing the remote. You sigh.

"It's Saturday night," you say.

"Yeah, I know, isn't it great?" he grins. "And tomorrow's Sunday, even better. Thanks for getting a sitter for the kids."

You bite your tongue. "Why did I get a sitter for the kids?" you ask.

"Great idea," he returns. "Wow, did you see that play?"

"I got a sitter so we could spend Saturday night together—just the two of us," you say, answering your own question through gritted teeth.

"We are spending Saturday night together," he says. "You wanna watch something different?"

"No!" you exclaim, at the end of your patience. "I want to go out! I don't want to stay here watching some dumb old TV program."

"Oh," he says, confused. "Why didn't you say so in the first place? All you had to do was ask."

"I don't want to have to ask! You're supposed to know!" you cry. "You're supposed to want to take me out, you're supposed to want to do something romantic on a Saturday night—it's Saturday night!" And off you run to sob into your pillow, wondering how you ended up with such an unfeeling, insensitive man who cares only about his pleasure and not a whit about yours.

What is it about having to ask for things that so rankles us? So much relationship misery is caused by women longing for their mates to say or do something romantic, and so much caused by men longing for their mates to say or do something sexy. Neither gender seems willing to ask for what he or she wants, yet relationships would fare much better if we did.

In the beginning, your new lover seems romantic because he's doing anything and everything he can think of to get you to like him. Once you're coupled, he figures (if only on a subconscious level) that you do like him and he doesn't have to do anything to "win" your love. He doesn't necessarily stop and think, "Of all the many things I tried in order to get her to like me, which ones worked? Which ones do I need to keep up?" He probably figures that just by being his ordinary self, and not seriously goofing up (lying, cheating, abusing), you'll be fine. His lack of romantic effort is *not* a measure of his love!

This is where we get ourselves seriously into trouble. You assume that because he isn't making a big fuss of Saturday night, or bringing you flowers, or remembering your mother's birthday, that he doesn't love you. He isn't doing those things because you're not asking for them on a regular basis. Going out on a Saturday night is important to you, not him. Flowers are nice to you, not him. And your mom's birthday... you get the drift.

Be willing to open your mouth and ask, "Sweetie, tomorrow night's Saturday night. I want us to go to dinner someplace nice, maybe go out to a club afterwards. Please make reservations at [insert name of favorite restaurant] for seven. I'm going to wear something really special and sexy—why don't you, too?" Be willing to check up and make sure he made those reservations. Be gracious about it. Don't resent having to ask. Don't resent having to ask more than once. Don't ask snidely, with sarcasm, or anything other than joy.

Be grateful you have a husband who, once asked, is willing to make those reservations, dress sexy, and take you out. The more you openly show your appreciation for his going along with your desires, the more likely it is he'll be happy to fulfill your wishes.

Who knows? After a few years of this, he may even start thinking of it himself.

Love is a fruit in season at all times, and within the reach of every hand.

—Mother Teresa

Unappreciated, Misunderstood, Taken for Granted

Finally, a Saturday night all to yourselves. You've been looking forward to this evening out with your husband for weeks. Coordinating your schedules, lining up the kids' events, and finding a sitter that won't bankrupt you was an awesome task, but hey, you were up to it. Now as you primp and ready yourself for what has to be a special evening, you look over to your husband, slumped on the living room couch in a channel-surfing daze, and ask, "Aren't you going to get dressed?"

"For what?" he replies, eyes never leaving the tube. "For our evening out," you say. "Don't tell me you've forgotten already."

Your husband can hear the warning in your voice and says, "No, of course not. Where are we going?"

"Where are we going?!" you cry. "What do you mean, 'where are we going'? You were the one who was supposed to make the plans. I did the kids, the schedule, the sitter, and everything else—you're incredible. I can't believe I married such a thoughtless, uncaring man," and off you go, mascara trailing woefully down your cheeks.

Locked in the bathroom, ignoring his "I'm sorry," you review your list of grievances. Not only did he forget your night out, but he never pays you compliments anymore, he complains about absolutely everything, his work/buddies/sports come before you every time, and listening to you consists mainly of saying "un-huh" distractedly every few sentences. Meanwhile you cook, clean, do most of the child care, and bring in a good portion of the bacon. You feel unappreciated, misunderstood, and taken for granted.

Well, before you file your divorce papers, have you ever wondered what your husband would say about his own feelings if caught in a candid moment when he wasn't worried about the consequences of speaking his mind? Probably that he too feels unappreciated, misunderstood, and taken for granted— just like you. Only being a guy, he may be less likely to articulate those feelings and more apt to resign himself to the feeling, "Well, that's marriage."

Well, that's not necessarily marriage. That's marriage where the daily, ongoing, outward expression of love has been neglected and fallen by the wayside. Yet that daily, ongoing, outward expression of love is easy to do and its rewards are amazing. It's good old-fashioned appreciation. You don't have to wait for your husband to appreciate you. Get the ball rolling by deliberately and consciously focusing on appreciating him.

This, of course, requires not caring who did what to whom, or who stopped appreciating first, or any other such pettiness. It means shedding your ego and valuing the health of your marriage and your happiness more than any finger-pointing or being "right."

Make a project of it. Find something to appreciate or be genuinely grateful for in every single interaction you have with your husband. For example: "Thank you for spending some time over breakfast with me"; "I love the way your skin feels"; "I'm grateful you're willing to work so hard to provide for me and the kids"; "Thanks for tanking up the car"; "I appreciate that you're willing to listen to me even when you're tired"; and a million other ways to appreciate him.

In short order, your husband will relax in the warm, loving feelings appreciation brings and look for ways to appreciate you. He may not use the exact words, he may not use words at all, but in his own way, whether it's by going along with your choice of a movie or minding the kids so you can have a few hours to yourself, he will be letting you know how very grateful he is to be married to such a loving wife.

Appreciating your sweetheart is natural in the beginning of a loving relationship. If you never let go of appreciation as the years go by, your love will burn brightly forever.

There is but one genuine love potion—consideration.
　　　　　　　　　　　　　　　　　　　—Menander

Getting Past the Defensive

You really are in a quandary. It seems that no matter what you say, your boyfriend responds defensively. You ask a perfectly civilized question, such as, "So what are your co-workers like?" or, "Did you talk to your supervisor about that problem you've been having?" and he says, "Why do you want to know?"

Well, that's not your favorite response, but you nevertheless continue with, "Did it ever occur to you I might be interested in who you work with?" or, "Don't you want me to be interested in what's going on with you?" But instead of giving you a straight answer, he gets angry with you. He accuses you of being intrusive, of prying, or of continually watching over his shoulder when that's truly not your intent.

The result is that instead of having a decent conversation, he goes off and broods in front of the TV, and you flounce off to the fridge to soothe your frustration. Neither of you is having any fun.

Yet you could be having fun again quite easily.

You see, it's often not what you say but *how* you say it that gets you into relationship difficulties. The way you're asking your question may very well be what's putting your boyfriend on the defensive. When you say, "Did it ever occur to you?" or, "Don't you want me to be interested?" you're implying that it should have occurred to him or that he should want you to be interested, which puts your boyfriend in the wrong. And no one likes to be put in the wrong.

Your boyfriend, now feeling attacked for not thinking of something he supposedly should have, lashes back at you, calling you "intrusive," which gets both of you nowhere. Avoid this entire unpleasant conversation simply by speaking more in "I" messages than in "you" messages. For example, when your boyfriend says, "Why do you want to know about my co-workers?" an "I" message would be something like: "Because I'm interested in your opinions of the people you're working with—what they're like, what you think of them."

Asking someone for their opinion is rarely confrontational. Most people enjoy giving their opinion. Similarly, when he says, "Why do you want to know if I talked to my supervisor?" an "I" message would be: "Because I know how important it is to you to do a good job, and I'm interested in whether your supervisor is giving you what you need to do that good job." Telling someone you are interested in their well-being and supportive of that well-being is equally non-confrontational.

As a general approach, phrasing questions in terms of where you're coming from ("I" messages) helps the other person feel more comfortable in answering you. You've already assured them that your questions are supportive, not demanding or critical. They are therefore more likely to answer you honestly, without hostility, and this will pave the way to further discussion. For example, accusing your boyfriend of being controlling when he refuses to go to "chick flicks" and only wants to see action films will likely put him on the defensive—"What's wrong with action films?! Those chick flicks are stupid." Instead, say something along the lines of: "I'm uncomfortable when I have only one option or alternative available to me. I'd like us to think of a couple of movies we both might enjoy." You will achieve a better result without either of you getting bent out of shape.

You don't have to be your boyfriend's clone in order to get along easily and have fun together. Learning to communicate effectively with each other may take some effort, but it's well worth the very pleasurable rewards.

Courage is what it takes to stand up and speak; courage is also what it takes to sit down and listen.

—Winston Churchill

Speaking to Our Inner Language

You stare belligerently at your husband. "This doesn't feel right," you say of the new couch cover he picked up on sale. "It's all rough and bumpy."

"Looks fine to me," he says. "It fits great."

"I know it fits," you reply. "I'm not talking about how it fits. I don't like the way it feels. It's uncomfortable."

"Picky, picky, picky," your husband says. "I can't do anything right by you," and off he stomps, sulking. You sigh.

Later, you're paying bills together. Your spouse proudly presents a new budget spreadsheet. You take one look at that thing and say, "I can't work with this, it's overwhelming! All those little boxes—how am I supposed to figure out what's what? My stomach is in knots just looking at it."

"What are you talking about?" your husband exclaims. "It's clear as can be—those boxes keep everything all lined up so you know what's what."

"I give up!" you cry. "It's like talking to a Martian—you don't understand a thing I say," and off you go, miserable, feeling terribly misunderstood and unappreciated, wondering how your marriage is going to survive if you can't communicate on the simplest of levels.

Why is it so difficult to get through to your husband? Why do you sometimes feel like you don't speak the same language at all? Because the truth is, you don't. Your husband does not understand you because you keep talking about how you *feel* about things, while your husband is talking about how things *look* to him. It's a classic male-female difference: many women often tend to relate first to things in terms of feeling, while certain men tend to relate to how something looks.

It's all about something called "perceptual modes," that is, the different ways each of us perceives things. You can perceive things visually (through your eyes), aurally (through your ears), or kinesthetically (through your physical sense of touch, or your emotional sense of feeling). Each of us uses all three modes, but many of us have a preference for one over the other; that preference is what determines our "inner" language—what you think and feel in first and foremost.

Many men are primarily visual, while many women are primarily kinesthetic. Of course there are exceptions, and lots of variations on the theme, including the fact that there are individuals who relate primarily to the world through their ears. The important thing isn't that "men are visual, women are kinesthetic"; it's that you must listen to your husband

(and others!) so you can determine which is *their* primary perceptual mode and then communicate in that way when you really want to get something across to them.

Detecting someone's perceptual mode is easy. We reveal our mode in the words we use to describe things. Your husband noticed that the couch cover "looks fine" and "fits great," both of which are visual terms. You complained of the "rough and bumpy" and "uncomfortable" texture, which are kinesthetic terms. Similarly, he noticed the spreadsheet boxes "lining up," while your stomach felt "knotted up" by them. Once you've determined a person's perceptual mode, express yourself accordingly.

Therefore, if you want to get through to your husband, try explaining your feelings in visual terms. For example: "The couch cover doesn't look right to me. It's got an uneven look to it," or, "The spreadsheet has too many little boxes for me, let's simplify the categories so there aren't so many of them."

When you talk your husband's inner language, you'll find his understanding of *you* increases exponentially.

Nothing in life is to be feared. It is only to be understood.
—Marie Curie

The Comparing Game

A new co-worker has joined the company. He's a breath of fresh air: young, energized, and always in an upbeat mood. You can hear his easygoing laugh as you sit at your work station, and it makes you smile every time.

You kiss your boyfriend "hello" when you get home at night, for you truly do love him, but you can't help noticing, as you're sitting there finishing off the last of the Chinese dinner you picked up on the way home, that he isn't particularly upbeat at the moment and doesn't laugh all that much. You shrug it off—he's probably just tired—and go about your evening ritual of TV, reading, flossing, and bed.

But the next day, you find yourself noticing even more your new co-worker's charming ways, and at night, noticing again how unlike your co-worker your boyfriend is. Over the weeks that follow, you continue this comparison game until finally you realize you're not in love with your boyfriend anymore at all, and break it off with him to begin dating your fun-loving young co-worker.

Everything is wonderful for awhile, but alas, the honeymoon phase ends, and guess what? You discover that your happy-go-lucky co-worker isn't always fun—as a matter of fact, he has downright depressed, moody days. And he doesn't always laugh that easy laugh; sometimes he doesn't laugh for days. You start to yearn for your old boyfriend, who was so kind and understanding, even if he wasn't the world's most upbeat person. You start to notice more and more about your new love that isn't quite as marvelous as you had thought.

You begin to think maybe you made a mistake. Then you start noticing the new bank teller, how intense his eyes are, and how winsomely he smiles at you as he hands over your cash. You're off and running into a new comparison game with an outcome that's all too easy to predict.

"What's wrong with me?" you ask. "Why can't I ever be satisfied in a relationship?"

"There's nothing wrong with you per se," I reply. "What's wrong is that you aren't looking for satisfaction."

You look at me, not comprehending. "Of course I'm looking for satisfaction, that's why I keep going from boyfriend to boyfriend," you say.

"No," I reply, "you're hoping satisfaction will drop in your lap. You're not looking for it at all."

You see, anything you focus on grows. If you are truly looking for satisfaction, then you deliberately focus on that which satisfies you. As you do, you will become even more satisfied. But you've been focused on comparing, using comparisons not with the intent to appreciate or grow the love you have, but to find fault, to find deficiency, thus guaranteeing that your dissatisfaction will grow. Truly, if you look for fault, you will find it, for none of us is perfect. We all come up short in various respects.

What to do? Don't compare, *appreciate*. Appreciate your co-worker's happy, upbeat personality. How nice, how delightful that he shares it with one and all. When you come home, appreciate your boyfriend for his qualities: he has lots of them, everybody does, and though they will be different from your co-worker's, it would be terribly boring if we lived in a cookie-cutter world.

It's a strange irony that we often stop appreciating those who are closest to us. We quit focusing on their good points and then blame them for the various flaws we start obsessing over and therefore magnify. If you want satisfaction, focus on what is satisfying about your relationship! Nurture that, value that, obsess over that, and it will grow to your great benefit.

Let what you admire about others remind you of the admirable traits you enjoy in your boyfriend. Stop playing the game of comparing, which only hurts and rarely has a happy ending.

What sunshine is to flowers, smiles are to humanity.
—Joseph Addison

Is the Honeymoon Over?

You had your toenails painted a bright iridescent blue—a radical departure from your usual conservative pale pink—and wiggle your bare toes happily when you're getting ready for bed. Does your husband notice? No, he just stays glued to the eleven o'clock news, even though nothing particularly earth-shattering is going on. You try harder. You put a foot between him and the TV, wiggle it around, and say, "Notice anything different?" And he says, "Huh? Could you put your foot down, Honey, I can't see the TV." So you do, and get into your side of the bed, angrily punching a place for your head in the pillow, feeling deprived and pouty.

You wonder what's changed since those wonderful early days when he worshipped the ground you walked on. You wonder why your friends, co-workers, and even the cashier at the supermarket will pay you compliments, while your husband never does. You remember how he used to compliment you all the time on all sorts of things—your perfume, a new hairstyle, or just how special you are to him—but now? You feel like you're an old shoe: comfortable, dependable, but not worth special attention.

You sigh. You know your husband loves you, but you figure, oh well, it must just be the way things are once the honeymoon is over. There's not much you can do about it, so you go to sleep, depressed.

What an unfortunate conclusion, and how unnecessary! There's a lot you can do about it. There is no reason for the sparkle in your relationship to die just because you aren't newly weds or newly shacked up. On the contrary, the bliss of a long-term relationship is that it can grow more loving and more rewarding over time. Committed partners can become increasingly special to each other as the years go by, not necessarily less so.

So how do you do it? How do you see to it that your relationship increases in delight through the years? But first, how do you get the compliments and attention you're so hungry for? By giving them, of course.

Remember when you first met? When you loved everything about him? When you hung on his every word and appreciated everything about him, from the way he walked and talked and looked to his views on current affairs? Re-create the feelings of those wonderful times by doing what you did then. Appreciate your husband. Praise him! Give him compliments, adoring looks, and tell him how much you value him.

Don't concern yourself with what you are getting

in return—don't give any thought to what you are getting or not getting—just go about the business of openly, verbally, vigorously appreciating your husband in every way you can think of.

Offer him words of praise. Give him kisses and hugs while you spend precious time together. Thank him for the smallest thing he does to help you. Listen to what is important to him. Respect his opinions even when you don't agree with him. Write him love notes and little Post-its—send him cards if that's what he would enjoy. Go about the business of really loving your husband with enthusiasm and passion.

Little by little, as you appreciate your spouse, he'll remember how to appreciate you. It may take some time, so be patient. But as you create a warm, loving, appreciative environment for him, he will naturally find himself doing the same for you. You can then begin the most wonderful phase of your relationship: the true "happily ever after."

Kindness in words creates confidence. Kindness in thinking creates profoundness. Kindness in giving creates love.
—Lao-Tzu

That Loving Feeling

You wake up in the middle of the night to the sound of your husband's snoring (for the thousandth time) and nudge him so he'll stop. He does, sweet soul that he is. But as you lie there, waiting to fall asleep again, you don't feel the usual "I'm so lucky to be in love with such a great guy" feeling. You feel—nothing. You figure, "Oh, well, I'm just tired," and think nothing of it. But the next morning, as you get up and go about your morning chores, you don't feel that special feeling as he hugs you. And as the week goes by, you gradually come to realize that you're not feeling that little catch in your throat or that special pleasure at just being together.

You worry. Are you no longer in love with your husband? Does not feeling "in love" mean your relationship is dead in the water? You're appalled. You thought the two of you would be together forever, but how can you stay with a man you're not in love with anymore?

134 — Dr. Noelle C. Nelson

Whoa—not so fast! There is being "in love," and then there is "loving." Being in love is a feeling, and as such, it comes and goes over the years. Loving someone is a lot more than the feeling of "being in love." Loving someone is a feeling *plus* a way of looking at someone with tenderness, kindness, and compassion. Loving someone is an intention, *and* it's an action—or many actions. Loving someone is caring about that person, being supportive of them, and being devoted to them. Loving is much more permanent than "being in love." Loving someone is something that grows and develops as you share your life together.

The bottom line is that "loving" is a *choice*; it's something you choose to do towards someone, whether or not you are feeling "in love" with the person at that particular moment in time. "Being in love" is a feeling that doesn't seem to have a whole lot to do with choice. It just arises, seemingly out of nowhere, and can seem to disappear just as suddenly. "Being in love," however, seems to flow quite predictably out of loving someone. It just isn't necessarily there all of the time.

This is good news. Just because you're not feeling all glowy and in love in the moment, it doesn't mean your relationship is over. It means it's time to focus on growing the loving—on growing the caring, support, compassion, and devotion to your husband that together form the foundation of a long-term relationship. The qualities that make up loving are what give your relationship emotional staying power over the long haul.

Any time you're not "in love," focus on appreciating what your husband contributes to your life and to the household. Focus on appreciating the person that he is. For example, deliberately notice, value, and be grateful for his willingness to help out with chores, his uncomplaining nature, the bills he pays. Notice, value, and be grateful for his good humor, his desire to improve himself, his easy way with friends.

As you make the choice to focus on appreciating whatever you can value about your husband, you are deepening the love between you. As you do, you'll find that "in love" feeling comes back surprisingly and delightfully time and time again.

Young love is a flame; very pretty, often very hot and fierce, but still only light and flickering. The love of the older and disciplined heart is as coals, deep, burning, unquenchable.
—Henry Ward Beecher

Un-Bratting a Brat

Y̲ou pick up your eleven-year-old from his friend's house after a weekend sleepover, and the friend's mom is praising your son to the skies, telling you what a fine child you have and how proud you must be. She's never had one of her son's playmates be such a help around the house, and she's positively gushing with compliments.

Your son is standing there, lapping it up, looking oh-so-humble and modest—meanwhile, you're seething. It's all you can do to keep a (completely fake) smile glued to your face as you listen, as you mutter a polite thank you, thinking, "Boy, does he have you fooled!" For you know the truth about your son. He may be a goody two-shoes when he's in someone else's house, but the minute he gets home, he's an obnoxious brat. He gives you major attitude and can usually be counted on to do the precise opposite of what you ask him.

Why can't he bring home some of that good

behavior instead of driving you crazy? More important, how do you put a stop to this Dr. Jekyll/Mr. Hyde act? It's simple, just use your son's good behavior outside of the home as leverage for getting him to behave inside your home. You see, whether or not you know it, your child is perfectly capable of good behavior. Otherwise, he wouldn't be exhibiting it around other people. The problem isn't that your son doesn't know how to be a responsible young person, but rather that he doesn't want to be when he's at home. Not wanting or resisting to do something always has a reason behind it. Your job is to discover what that reason is.

Your natural desire may be to scold him, to ask, "Why can't you be good when you're at home? Why do you turn into a complete brat?" This will not, however, give you a reason you can work with. Your child is most likely to respond with something like: "Because I hate you," or "Because you're so mean"— neither of which is very helpful. Instead, look for the positive in your son by adopting a positive approach. Sit down with your child when you're both fairly relaxed and getting along well. Start by telling him, "Honey, I'm so proud of you—people tell me all the time what a terrific kid you are and how helpful you are when you're at their house. So I'm curious, what makes it easier for you to be on good behavior when you're away from home?"

This approach will work best if it's genuine, if you are truly interested in your child's lack of motivation, as opposed to wanting merely to prove yourself right. Children know perfectly well when we're "faking it," and they don't like it.

The next step: listen. Resist the urge to defend or justify—just listen. If you're willing to wait a while and let your child get his thoughts out in his own good time, you may be surprised at what you hear. Children often feel they aren't praised for good behavior, only bawled out when they mess up—so why bother being good? Other times, kids feel that what they do in terms of contributing to the household chores is taken for granted or discounted, and that doesn't feel right to them either. Sometimes children feel that their parents are inconsistent both in what is asked of them and in how they are rewarded or punished.

Whatever the reason, take it seriously. Let this be the beginning of an ongoing conversation with your child where both of you learn more about each other's motivations and expectations. What you'll find is that your children are much more willing to listen to you when you're willing to listen to them, and from there, anything is possible.

Appreciation is a wonderful thing: it makes what is excellent in others belong to us as well.

—Voltaire

Ah, the Holidays

The holidays are here, and what do we think of? Some time off—yay! Parties, family gatherings, special times with friends, and gift giving. Lots and lots of gift giving, and of course some gift receiving. All of this to be done in a spirit of Happy Holiday Celebration.

This despite the fact that your time off is never enough (you have a holiday to-do list that even Martha Stewart would find daunting) and parties throw you into a tizzy of "I don't have anything to wear" and "What if my ex shows up?" You dread having to clean up the house/spouse/kids/pets/garden for the inevitable visits from relatives ("Oh, you'd like to stay for two weeks?!") who are bound to find something wrong with something (you don't know what, but you dread it anyway). Of course there's the round of malls, stores, catalogues, and online shopping to do as you desperately seek the perfect gift for a seemingly unending list of people in the full-on crush of traffic, other shoppers, and kids out of school. Let's not even mention the status of your credit cards. Ah, the holidays... Maybe you can make like a bear and hibernate through the whole thing.

And yet there's something wonderful about the holidays. Even through the frenzy of it all, there's an excitement about them, a feeling of something magical going on that catches you up short and makes you smile. Even if you hate the holidays, you hate them precisely because you know there's something magical about this time of year, and somehow you're not in the loop. That hurts.

You see, the holidays (whichever ones you observe) are a time of celebration. It doesn't matter what your faith or cultural tradition is, the holidays are a time to rejoice, to praise, to glorify, to exalt. The key to truly enjoying the holidays in spite of your many holiday obligations is to accomplish as many of your tasks as possible in a spirit of rejoicing and praise.

Tackle your holiday to-do list with zeal: "How wonderful that I have some time to do this! I'm proud of myself for getting going on this list." Don't criticize yourself (okay, so that's too mild—don't *beat up* on yourself) when you only get through the first two items. Step back and look lovingly on what you *did* accomplish. Praise yourself and the job you did; enjoy the satisfaction of what you *did* do.

Assume that your relatives are going to complain about something regarding the house/your cooking/the sleeping arrangements/your children's upbringing so that you can quit trying to revamp your entire life around occasional visitors—relatives or no—and focus on pleasing yourself. Celebrate the happiness that is your home, your spouse, your kids, and your cooking by arranging things to your satisfaction. Of course you want things to be pleasant for your visitors or dinner guests, but within reason! Obsessing over what Aunt Edith is going to think of your failure to use antimacassars, or what Cousin Henry is going to think of your less-than-100-year-old Scotch just doesn't come under the category of rejoicing. Instead, extol the virtues of what you *do* choose to offer, rejoice in your heart over the goodness of your hearth and home that permits you to welcome the people who come celebrate with you.

Let your gift giving be what gift giving is meant to be: an honoring of people, a way to praise and extol the virtues of your friends and family, co-workers, employees, employers, and whomever else you choose to give to. Gift giving should not be an eye-for-an-eye sort of thing: "I have to give my boss a very expensive gift because she's my boss." Gift giving in the true spirit of celebration is giving someone something they would truly enjoy—something that honors them as a unique person, be it a $5.95 paperback book, a $59.95 hour at the local spa, or a $599.95 antique footstool! Teach your children that holiday gift receiving isn't simply about getting: the holidays are about honoring people for who they are. Teach your kids this one early on and you'll save yourself a lot of, "But Mommy, Tommy got one, why can't I?" down the road.

Let the holidays become a genuine time of

rejoicing, celebration, and praise, and they will resound with laughter, full of magic and great joy.

Know the true value of time—snatch, seize and enjoy every moment of it.

—Lord Chesterfield

Getting It Done "Right"

You tell your thirteen-year-old, "Go clean up your room."

"I'm busy," she replies, painting her toenails.

"Too bad. Go clean it now."

"Why?" she retorts, blowing a blue pinkie dry. "You never like the way I do it anyway."

"What are you talking about?" you ask.

"You go in there after me and do it all over again."

"Well that's 'cause you miss stuff. You don't clean thoroughly."

"See—that's what I mean. No matter what I do—it's not right," and off she stomps, leaving you confused and frustrated.

You ask your husband to clean out the garage. He says, "No way, not by myself."

You say, "Honey—for Heaven's sake, I've got the kids' practice to go to and I promised my mom I'd help her go shopping this weekend—you can handle it by yourself."

He stands firm: "Nope. You want the garage cleaned out, you be here for it."

"Why, what's the big deal?"

"Because I won't do it right," he snorts. "You'll come back from your mom's, take one look at what I've done, and do it all over again yourself." You stand there, flummoxed. That's the second time you've heard that today. Now that you think about it, you hear that a lot. You wonder, "What's wrong with wanting things done right?"

Nothing, in the abstract. But you're defeating your own purpose, both with your child and your spouse, by forgetting the people involved. How you go about getting things done "right" is as important as getting them done.

For example, your teen may have an attitude, but what she says has a lot of truth to it—you're forgetting that your thirteen-year-old is a child, still learning. When you take one look at her idea of a good cleaning job and immediately redo it, you're implying that she is incompetent. This is highly demoralizing, especially given that your daughter is at a stage in her life where she's going through many changes and she's not feeling all that secure as it is. And here you come along, giving her every reason to feel even less secure.

Instead, when you go to check on how well your teen cleaned her room, praise her for what she did right: "Great job! The bed looks nice and neat, and your bathroom mirror is positively shining." Ignore the dust bunnies under the bed and in the corner; no one is going to die from a few dust bunnies. The following week, show her how to use the vacuum attachment to get at the elusive dust, and don't say a word about her having missed the dust the week before. The more you simply praise and teach, the more willingly your child will cooperate.

With your husband, the feeling of being incompetent is just as hurtful, although usually for different reasons. He wants nothing more than to please you, and when he fails to do so, he feels inept and, to a degree, humiliated. Just because you're not outright saying, "You're doing it wrong," it doesn't make your displeasure any less obvious—redoing someone's task clearly demonstrates your disapproval. Either clean out those areas which are important to you yourself and be willing to accept your husband's version of cleaning out the rest of the garage as good enough, or set aside a time when you can do it together. Whichever you choose, don't think him wrong for doing a task his way.

Getting things done your way may feel very satisfying, but when it's at the expense of your family's happiness, it's hardly worth it. Take your family's feelings into account and you'll all feel a lot better about "getting it done right."

To improve is to change; to be perfect is to change often.
—Winston Churchill

Young Love

You're so proud of your daughter. Here she is starting college, holding down a part-time job, saving up so she can move into her own place, all at the tender age of eighteen—you positively beam with pride at the forward-thinking levelheadedness of your first-born. The future is wide open in front of her, everything is possible, and yet she is inexplicably smitten with a boyfriend—a part-timer at the local 7-11 who plays a little rock and roll on the side, lives with his parents, and has no plans for his future—who clearly isn't Mr. Ambitious (or anything else, as far as you are concerned).

You could cry. His only redeeming feature is a relative lack of skin art. You cringe for your daughter. You don't want her ruining her life and so you try to ease gently into a "dump this creep" conversation.

"You should date more, sweetie, you're too young to settle down," you say.

"Mom," your daughter replies, instantly on

guard, "why can't you just say it—you don't like my boyfriend."

"I like him just fine," you say, faking it as best you can. "I just don't think he's..." you peter out. How can you say "not husband material" of your child's true love?

"What?" your daughter snaps. "Up to your standards?"

"Well," you begin, taking a deep breath and going for it, "you could do better. Before I met your father, I dated a lot of guys and—"

"Mom!" your daughter says, interrupting, "I'm not you, okay?" and she stomps off leaving you to wonder why she won't listen to you when you try to guide her and help her through life. What's so wrong about wanting the best for her?

Nothing. Every parent wants the best for their child, but by the time your daughter is eighteen years old, she is very much her own person, not an extension of you. Your child is sorting out who she is, and that includes her preferences in boyfriends. Just as you figured out (eventually) who would be right for you, trust that your daughter will too. If you want to protect and guide her, you're going to have to do it more as you would with a *friend*, not as with the child she used to be.

This being said, guidance is important. With a friend, you might jokingly say, "Well he's not your usual cup of tea," or more seriously, "I'm not sure he's good for you," and leave it be. With your daughter, you still have the natural and appropriate desire to influence her decisions towards what you feel are good choices. You do need to voice your opinion on her boyfriends and other important life matters in more specific terms than you might feel comfortable doing with a friend.

How do you do it?

1) Say what you have to say in straightforward fashion.

If you were speaking with a good friend, you wouldn't try to manipulate them by saying, "You should date more," instead of what you mean ("I don't think your boyfriend is good for you.") Treat your daughter in like fashion. Don't drop hints or skirt the issue or try to creep up on it. Instead, set aside a time to talk, and be direct: "Honey, I will welcome whomever you choose to love, however, I also have my opinion. Here are my concerns about your boyfriend." Lay it out for her—once—and then let it go.

2) Accept her response.

Accept your daughter's response. She may not say anything at all. Let that be all right. If she does respond, listen courteously, and don't argue. Say simply (and sincerely), "I respect your opinion." Be willing to change the subject, as in, "So, would you like to go to lunch?" and move on to something else.

Your daughter is fast becoming an adult. Respect her as such—and watch the friendship between you blossom.

In love you find the oddest combinations: materialistic people find themselves in love with idealists; clingers fall in love with players; homebodies capture and try to smother butterflies. If it weren't so serious we could laugh at it.
—George Davis

Those Moving Blues

You have to move. Whether your job requires it, your lease is up, or you've finally found the home of your dreams, you have to move. Your six-year-old is thrilled! All he can talk about is starting school, the fun bugs he found the day you visited, and the dog you promised he can have—well, maybe. Your teenage daughter, however, is behaving like you're destroying her life. All you hear from her is, "I'll never see my friends again, I have to go to a new school, you're horrible and I hate you!" Par for the course.

The one who has you the most mystified is you! You are every bit as cranky and ornery as your teen, yet you know full well this is a necessary move. You don't want to lose your job, and a transfer was the only way to a promotion; or if it's your lease that was up, well heck, you were tired of the old place anyway. Of course, if you're moving to the home of your dreams, you're even more confused. Why aren't you dancing for joy like your six-year-old?

You know that moving is stressful, but that's about the logistics: cleaning out and packing and schlepping and organizing and travelling. It's a nuisance, but it doesn't account for your cranky, depressed self. What gives?

Moving represents change, and no matter how desirable, change is stressful, if not downright painful. There's a great deal of comfort in what is familiar to us. We trust what we know, we fear what we don't know.

Make your new environment familiar to you. If you can, pack the kids in the car and take an afternoon to drive around your new neighborhood before the actual move. Locate the cleaners, the market, the coffee place, the library—whatever would be typical places you would go to on a regular basis. Walk into each establishment, take a look around, say "hello," let people know you'll be the "new kid" on the block. If you're moving too far away for a drive to be practical, take a virtual stroll around your new area via the Internet. Many communities have websites, and local realtors often include neighborhood information on their homepages.

Moving also entails uprooting relationships. This is why your teenager is suffering the torments of the damned. Relationships are crucial to teenagers—especially to girls. In your daughter's mind, you are destroying her life. The group of friends she so painstakingly cultivated, the hangouts she's marked as her own, the few adults she has come to trust—in her mind, are all being ripped from her, and you don't seem to care one bit.

To ease your daughter's distress, start by acknowledging it. Say to her, "Honey, you're right. This feels awful. You are having to give up so much of what you're used to—I'm sorry." Then give her suggestions on how to keep in touch with her most precious friends. Offer to help her out by driving her wherever she needs to go, or by arranging holiday get togethers. Once your teenager sees that you take her distress seriously, she will feel less like you're deliberately betraying her. This will make her adjustment— and yours—easier.

A teen isn't the only one with relationships. Whether you loved or hated your old neighborhood, you had relationships there too. Take some time to appreciate those relationships for what they meant to you; let yourself feel the sadness of leaving behind those which must be left behind. It's natural to feel a period of loss and mourning. Be gentle with yourself and allow yourself to feel the longing for what was, without letting it interfere with your interest in the good that is to come.

Make arrangements to continue the relationships you want to keep. E-mail, camera phones, and other technology make keeping up with loved ones much easier. Be proactive in creating relationships in your new neighborhood: join the local gym, go to PTA meetings, attend the local church or temple, introduce yourself to neighbors.

Moving can be an exciting, stimulating, renewing event in your life. Keep looking forward to the many new people you'll meet, the places you'll discover, and the positive experiences you'll have and you'll soon feel the many blessings of your new neighborhood.

Happiness is essentially a state of going somewhere, whole-heartedly, one directionally, without regret or reservation.
—William Sheldon

Unwanted, Unsolicited "Advice"

You love your mom dearly, and given the fact that you're a fully grown adult whose life runs pretty well with relatively few disasters and crises, you don't understand why she is forever telling you what to do. Worse yet, you feel guilty when you oppose her and insist on doing things your way.

For example, your mom says, "You really should-n't wear orange, dear. It makes you look sallow."

You cringe. "I like orange, Mom. I don't think it makes me look sallow."

"Well, dear, have you looked at yourself? It does," Mom says, promptly pulling out her compact and shoving it your way. "Look."

"I don't want to look," you reply. "I know what I look like, okay?"

"I'm just telling you for your own good. Surely you don't want to look sallow?"

"Mom! Sallow is fine, okay?"

"Of course, dear," she sighs.

Now you've done it. Your mom is all upset, but what to do? You can't dress to please her or you'd be in beige permanently.

Of course, your mom's "advice" doesn't stop at what you should wear—that'd be too easy. She freely informs you how to behave towards your spouse, raise your kids, handle your finances, and pretty much lectures you on everything else in life. It really doesn't matter what the subject is, you never agree with her. And since you can only listen to so much of this, you end up upsetting her and making yourself feel guilty. Eventually, you spend less and less time with your mom in order to avoid these situations, but that doesn't make you feel good either.

Then there's your best friend, who liberally tells you you're reading all the wrong books, listening to all the wrong music, and that you'll never be "in the groove," as if being "in the groove" mattered to you anyway! Too much of the time you spend with your friend makes you feel uncomfortable and somehow dysfunctional, when in truth, you love your friend and don't want to lose the friendship.

Of course you don't. And you certainly don't want to lose the benefit of your relationship with your mom either, just to avoid the discomfort of these interactions.

Fortunately, there is a way to handle such "advice."

1) Appreciate the input.

As odd as it may seem, most people who proffer unsolicited advice are content so long as they feel that they've been heard. A simple (but sincere) "Thank you for telling me that," or "Thank you. I appreciate your concern," can be very effective.

If you can't be grateful for the actual advice given (which is likely), just focus your gratitude on the fact that this person cares enough about you to want good things for you. When you focus on the caring instead of on your disagreeing with the advice given to you, your thanks can be genuine.

2) Change the subject.

Once you've acknowledged appreciation for the input offered by your mom or your friend, change the subject. Do not give the other person an opportunity to elaborate on their advice. That's where you've gotten yourself into trouble in the past.

Become an expert at changing the subject. Always have on hand two or three easy ways to move the conversation into a different direction. This doesn't take a rocket scientist—something as simple as "Did you see that fantastic recipe for peach pie in the paper this morning?" or, "I wonder when the weather is going to change; it's been awfully [hot/cold/snowy]," or "I've been reading a terrific new author lately," will do nicely.

Expressing gratitude for advice and changing the subject allows you to steer clear of that uncomfortable discussion which otherwise leaves your mom or friend feeling unappreciated and you feeling guilty. To top it off, there's a happy ending: you enjoy the company of your mom and your friend so much more!

A loving heart is the truest wisdom.

—Charles Dickens

"You're Right"

You're in yet another argument with your spouse. You want a new washer-dryer; he says there's not enough money. You point out you're wasting time and money nurse-maiding the old one along through repair after repair. He yells, insisting that he's doing the best he can and wondering why that's never good enough. You both storm off, terribly unhappy with each other.

And then there's the predictable weekly argument over chores: you want him to do more, he wants to do less. You point out that you're already doing most of the housework and that all he does on Sunday afternoons is veg in front of the TV or the computer. He retorts that if he doesn't get some downtime, he's gonna explode, and he asks if you'd rather he camp out at a bar. You sigh, you give up—of course you don't want him at a bar! You do the rest of the chores.

Or there's your teenagers... talk about arguing!

They are absolute masters of the art. You say curfew is at midnight, they say you're an inhuman monster. You tell them to do their homework now, they spend the next hour arguing with you over why they can't do it now. It's not long before you're totally exhausted, wondering if you know how to parent at all, and just tell them in no uncertain terms to do what you said because you said it, which leads to hours of their sulking, pouting, slamming of doors, and generally unpleasant behavior.

You feel as if you can't win. Somehow, whenever you argue with your family members, even if you get your way, it doesn't feel good. But you don't want to give in to their every wish and preference, roll over and play dead. How do you resolve this? By learning to say, "You're right." This is not giving in to their every wish and preference, but it is part of a strategy that can break the argument cycle and lead to real results.

In a nutshell, the strategy is to refuse to defend. Go straight to problem solving. You see, it takes two to argue. Even when you argue with yourself, you have to talk from two sides of you. Petty arguments don't work. Petty arguments aren't persuasive.

Arguments typically end because someone gives in—usually out of exhaustion or fear—but nothing gets resolved because there's no mutual decision-making. That's why the same old argument crops up again and again.

Instead, here's what to do:

1) When an argument starts, put yourself on red alert.

Stop everything and listen.

2) Find something in what the other person says that you can agree with.

There is always some aspect you can agree with. For example, if your spouse is yelling about never having enough money, say, "You're right. I want more money too."

3) Enjoy the silence.

Invariably, when you say "you're right" to someone who expects you to argue with them, you will get a lovely moment of silence.

4) Find a solution.

Jump right in there and say, "Let's each write down some ideas about how this situation could be resolved, and let's set a time to sit down and work it out." Now you have a chance to negotiate your different positions so you can arrive at a solution that works for both of you.

Arguments don't have to be the bane of your family life. Feel the power of "you're right" and stop the argument cycle before it ever even gets started.

Don't find fault. Find a remedy.

—Henry Ford

The Power of Appreciation
with Work and Money

Dealing with the New Boss

After months of negotiations and much fanfare, your company has merged with another company. The higher-ups have reassured all of you that business will go on as usual and that there'll be a minimum of restructuring and reorganization. Your jobs are safe.

Right. You've heard that one before. Only last month, your best friend got dumped after eleven years with her company! You were appalled. She just looked at you with weary eyes and said, "What did you expect? That new management would embrace a bunch of us they didn't hire and can't control like they will new hires? Get real." You blessed your stars you weren't in her position, and guess what? Now you are.

So you worry yourself sick; you hardly sleep for thinking about it all night. "I will get canned, won't I? How will I pay the rent? Where would I get another job? What about my pension? I'll lose everything!" Your stomach churns so badly when you go to work that you're going through a bottle of Tums a day. You get nervous at the very sight of your new boss. You've bitten your nails down to the quick. Every time your boss comes up to say something to you, your heart palpitates. "Now?" you think. "Is he going to can me now?"

Your friends remind you that you survived the last turnover, but that doesn't reassure you. That was eight years ago, when you were in a lower position and didn't care all that much whether you stayed or went. Since then, you've been promoted systematically, your pay is good, your benefits precious. You knew management well—they liked you and you liked them. You worry that this boss won't like you. What if he has something against short people, or brunettes, or different ethnicities, or who knows what?! You get a headache just thinking about it. You mutter, "I gotta make him like me, I gotta make him like me," like some sort of New Age mantra, as if that were the answer.

Unfortunately, it's not. Life is not a popularity contest, and whether your new boss likes you is hardly the issue. What's important is whether your new boss comes to value you, which is to say, to recognize your ability and worth to him. Fortunately, there's a lot you can do about that.

Start by getting your priorities straight. You're looking at the situation backwards: instead of worrying about whether your new boss will like you, focus on getting to know him, not personally, but as a boss, someone you work with as well as for. How do you do that? Do your research. What department did he manage previously? What was his management style? How can you best work within that style? Find out what your boss accomplished in his previous position, what he was proud of doing. This will tell you something about what matters to your boss. Then you can make that important to you.

Get to know your new boss' key goals and objectives. Find out what he wants to accomplish on a daily or weekly basis. Figure out how you can best help him reach his goals. And tell him! Your boss is just as anxious about doing a good job in his new position as you are about keeping your current one. At this point, you know your job far better than he does. When you say to your boss, "Here are some of the ways I've thought of that I can help you achieve your objectives," you are being of enormous benefit to him: he doesn't have to figure out from scratch how best to fit your duties to his goals.

Communicate openly and directly with your boss. Let him know what you need from him or other members of his team in order to do your very best for him. Be willing to hear his comments and suggestions about how to do things differently without getting defensive or upset. Listen attentively and be open to new ways of doing things.

Lastly, do a good job. Be prompt and thorough so that your boss learns to rely on the quality of your work. He'll be hard pressed to dump you when you're coming through so well for him.

A wise man will make more opportunities than he finds.
—Francis Bacon

Too Sensitive

Your supervisor throws a sheaf of papers onto your desk and stands there, hands on hips, yelling at you: "What's wrong with you? This is a piece of crap. Do it over. Now." You feel yourself turning crimson from the shame and embarrassment; you know everybody's listening. You fight back the tears that threaten to spill over. You say, "Yes Sir," and pick up the pages, trembling.

Ten minutes later, the department head comes up to you and says, "These requisitions aren't filled out properly." You burst into tears. "Well it's not that bad," your department head says, mystified by your ragged sobs. "You just put in the wrong code. Boy, are you sensitive," she says as she leaves. Your co-worker at the next desk takes pity on you and comes over with a box of tissues. "It's a job—don't sweat it. You know the super yells at everybody. You're just too sensitive."

"Too sensitive"! You've heard that all your life.

What is that supposed to mean and what are you supposed to do about it? You feel what you feel—you can't help that!

Indeed, you feel what you feel. Feelings, however, don't come out of the blue. Feelings come out of the *meaning* you give to any event. For example, your nose is stuffy, you have a fever, you cough. If you say to yourself, "Oh, darn, another cold," you're simply irritated at the inconvenience. If instead you say to yourself, "Oh, no, I've got pneumonia," you're afraid that your health may be in serious danger.

When you feel shame and embarrassment from your supervisor yelling at you, it's because the *meaning* you're giving to his yelling might be: "I'm bad, I'm wrong, I'm a terrible employee." You're not recognizing that his yelling and the way he is asking you to redo a piece of work are entirely inappropriate. He is personally attacking you, and that is not acceptable in the workplace.[1] The one who should feel shame and embarrassment is your supervisor, not you.

The meaning that would be more accurate to give to his comments is: "Oh, he didn't like how I did this piece of work. Okay. Let me find out what I need to do, and do it the way he wants it done."

By the time your department head made an entirely appropriate request, you were unfortunately still hurt and vulnerable from your supervisor's yelling and took her request as yet more "proof" of what a terrible employee you are.

Your feelings are your feelings, yes. Your feelings are precious and valuable responses to the world around you. Protect your feelings by paying more attention to the meaning that you give to the events and situations you experience.

If you have trouble giving different meanings to hurtful situations, ask friends you trust how they would feel under the same circumstances and what meanings they would give to the event. Shift the meaning you give to previously hurtful events and you'll find you will hurt a lot less.

There is nothing either good or bad, but thinking makes it so.
—William Shakespeare

---

[1]Please note that in addition to the suggestions given in this chapter, any ad hominem, abusive personal attacks by co-workers or your employer should be documented and reported to the human resources department or to other appropriate personnel.

Be Careful What You Wish For

You have longed for, worked for, and finally received that big promotion at work. You're thrilled, jumping up and down for joy, and then it hits you: what if you can't handle the new responsibility?

Or, you gave presentation upon presentation to a prospective client, wooed the client persistently over many months, and—presto!—the client is yours. You rejoice, ecstatic, until it dawns on you: you actually have to service this account. Getting it was just the beginning, now you have to fulfill all your promises.

Or maybe you made a courageous decision to go into an entirely new line of work. You studied hard, learned the skills, made the rounds, and landed that new job. Only now, you sit there with a pile of instructions, manuals, duties, and files, fresh out of your orientation meeting, wondering what you've gotten yourself into and how fast you're gonna sink before (if ever) you learn to swim.

Be careful what you wish for, some would say. Yet the wiser course would be to say, "Now that you have what you wished for, plan for its success!" Getting what you want is only the beginning. It's like moving to a new city or landing in a foreign country: getting there is your starting point, not your ending point. When you panic about whether you're in over your head, what you're really doing is confusing your starting point with the finish line. So take a deep breath and get ready to start where you are, which is to say, at the beginning.

Planning for success is largely a matter of figuring out what your resources are and where you can get the help you need to be successful. Oh, you thought you had to go this alone? Heavens, no! This is your first lifeline—you are rarely alone in anything, unless you want to be.

Your first resource is the person who hired or promoted you. Thank them for this terrific opportunity and tell them just how well you want to do what you've been hired to do. Ask for the names of all those who can assist you in learning about the company and the ins and outs of your job. Write those names down even as you sit there.

Next, go to every one of those people, introduce yourself and thank them ahead of time for the help you may be asking them for. And as it becomes appropriate, ask them! People enjoy being asked for their advice (as long as you don't overdo it) and are usually more than willing to help out a newbie. Be sure to express your appreciation.

Other available resources might include co-workers, work-related organizations and profession-al associations, trade magazines, books and journals, seminars, classes, and the omnipresent Internet.

And then, of course, there's your attitude. When you focus on what can go wrong, you end up finding it and usually land in a sea of problems you could have easily avoided. Search for the silver lining instead. Focus on the fact that your employer obviously has faith in your abilities and will be patient as you get yourself up to speed. Focus on your abilities yourself: remind yourself that you have the smarts, the savvy, the persistence, the motivation, and the courage to do a good job. Focus on how helpful everybody is likely to be when you come up against something you don't know how to handle. Look for what can go right and things are a lot less likely to go wrong.

"Be careful what you wish for" will become "I'm so glad I wished for it!" as you enjoy your well-deserved success.

The future belongs to those who prepare for it.
—Ralph Waldo Emerson

Cellphone/Pager Hell

You're having a quiet dinner out, just the two of you. The kids are parked at your in-laws, you don't even have to call home to check up on them: what a treat. You're just starting on a scrumptious Caesar salad, when your pager vibrates. You try to ignore it, but the thing won't quit. It feels like an elf with a jackhammer thudding at your waist. Finally, you say, "Excuse me," and take a look at who's calling.

"Work?" your spouse asks sweetly.

"Who else?" you reply, pulling out your cellphone.

You try to be discreet, since there's nothing you hate more than people yakking loudly on their cells in public places. Your boss, who clearly doesn't have a life, wants something else done tomorrow in addition to the already impossible number of items you're to attend to between 9 and 5. Fine. You turn your attention back to your sweetheart, and that delicious salad. Peace and pleasant conversation reign. For ten whole minutes. Then—*bzzz*—there goes that elf at your waist again. Same drill: pager—cellphone—boss. "Couldn't wait until you got in to work tomorrow, huh?" your spouse says, a little less sweetly.

"Apparently not," you reply.

Later when you're in the car on your way home, your cellphone rings. This time it's a client who seems to think conducting business at 10 p.m. is perfectly normal. You try to keep the conversation as short as possible, but you see from your spouse's white-knuckled grip on the steering wheel that they're not too pleased with the interruption. "Work," you say meekly.

"I know," your spouse responds through gritted teeth.

Finally, just as the car pulls up to your home, your cell rings that annoying Beethoven's Fifth again, which you thought was so neat at the time, and the love of your life says, "I've had it—you're not married to me, you're married to your work!" and slams out of the car, your romantic evening now completely ruined. You're crushed. But what can you do? You gotta work!

What happened? How did your 9 to 5, Monday through Friday work week turn into a nonstop 24/7/365 drill? When did you turn into a total slave to your work?

The short answer: since the advent of the cellphone and the pager. We used to be reachable only when located near a physical telephone. You had to be at your desk, at home, or by a payphone. That was pretty much it. Your boss couldn't reach you when you were running errands, in your car, at a restaurant, or at the soccer field. It made it much easier to separate work from your personal and family life.

Since cellphones and pagers have become standard equipment in the work world, work has entered arenas that used to be considered sacred and untouchable. Bosses and clients are only too happy to get ahold of you whenever it pleases them. If you want your personal and family time to be your own, it's up to you to deliberately make the division between work and your personal time.

Manage your electronic gizmos so that you are in control of your time, and not vice versa. Set appropriate boundaries so that work once again becomes a part of your life, not all of your life. For example, once you're on your own time, put your work beeper on call forwarding to a voicemail. Same with your cellphone. Check your messages once in the evening, just in case something truly urgent did come up, and that's that. Once your bosses and clients realize you are not available at their beck and call, they will begin to respect your personal time as such. You'll still be responsive to your work duties, you'll just no longer be married to them.

Then you will finally be able to have that scrumptious Caesar salad with your beloved spouse in blissful peace.

Time is the most valuable thing anyone can spend.
                                                    —Diogenes

The Job "Love Affair"

You've had the same job for five years now. You have no real complaints; after all, you're one of the lucky ones—you have a job! And a good job at that, with decent pay, decent benefits, and even a decent boss. So what's wrong with you? No matter how pleasant and restful your weekend was, it's all you can do to drag yourself to work on Monday morning. The day seems to go on and on, and those last minutes before five o'clock stretch out forever.

Yet somehow, once you're home, you're energized again, feeling fine. At least until the next morning, when it's all you can do to haul yourself into the shower and out the door. By Friday, you're thinking of calling the doctor for an antidepressant—you feel like that little sad round face in the Zoloft commercials, but you forget about it by Saturday morning when suddenly you're awake before the alarm clock, bright eyed and bushy tailed. Finally, you're forced to admit it: there's nothing wrong with you; there's something wrong with the combination of you and your job.

Why did the love affair with your job end? What happened to those glorious days when you looked forward to going to work, when you hardly noticed the hours flying by, when you found yourself jotting down ideas for one project or another on your way home?

It ended for the same reason most love affairs end: because you stopped giving to your job, and you stopped appreciating what your job gives to you.

"Not so!" you cry. "I give five days a week, a full forty hours, more like sixty some of the time. How much more can I give?!" But that's not the kind of giving that matters. It's not the number of hours you put in that makes your job enjoyable, it's the energy and commitment you give to it.

Too often we go into our jobs thinking, "I gotta do this, I gotta do that," which results in pressure and unrest, a condition not conducive to feeling good. Instead, take some time when you first get there to ask yourself what you want to accomplish today, and pick the one or two things that are important to *you* to accomplish.

Do these preferred tasks first, with as much pleasure and gusto as you can. Then sit back for a moment and enjoy the feeling of accomplishment. It doesn't matter if those one or two things are making a cold call to a prospective client or doing the research for that gigantic report that's due. What matters is that these things are what make you feel good about your work. You are giving yourself to your work instead of forcing yourself into it. Now you'll be more willing to tackle the other parts of your workday that are less pleasurable.

Appreciating what your work gives to you is the other part of this equation. Your paycheck is what undoubtedly comes first to mind, but what about everything else that work makes possible? For example, work stretches your brain by challenging you to develop new skills and to communicate with different types of people. Work gives you friends, if you choose to make them, as well as a sense of being productive by contributing to your community and society. Work gives you a way to express your talents, your opinions, and your perspective on things. Work helps define who you are and allows you to expand what you are about.

Take some time at the end of every day to express appreciation for what work has given you that day. Be specific! Say things to yourself like, "I appreciate that I resolved that conflict with my team members"; "I am grateful for the compliment my supervisor gave me"; "I appreciate that I was able to hold my tongue and not lash out at my co-worker"; "I am grateful for the opportunity to keep learning." Whatever it may be, appreciation will increase your sense of joy in your job and with that, your overall sense of satisfaction.

Work is a valuable and important part of life. When your love affair with your job lags, don't be so quick to forget the good times! Revitalize your relationship with your work by giving to it and appreciating what it gives to you. You'll once again be energized and happy—the only way to really be.

Happiness is not in strength, or wealth, or power, or in all three. It lies in ourselves...

—Epictetus

Get Your Nose off the Grindstone

Your alarm goes off—too early, much too early. As you struggle your way out of your warm, comfy nest, you say to yourself, "Another day, another grind," and off you go to the land of work. It doesn't matter what kind of work, whether in an office, a factory, a household, or on a spaceship, you'd love—no, let's rephrase that—you'd be *utterly ecstatic*, if you didn't have to work at all, if you could get off that work treadmill. Forever. But life, it seems, just isn't going to let you get away with that one. You're years away from retirement (if that ever becomes a reality) and somehow you don't think the bill collectors are going to forget to collect their money.

It's not that you have a bad job—you don't. It's not that you're ungrateful for the income—you are. It's not even that you don't like your boss, your co-workers, or customers—they're fine. So why, you ask, do you feel like you're being dragged through your 9 to 5 one weary day at a time, your only relief being that magic moment when you call it quits for the day?

Why do you feel this way? Because you've lost your sense of purpose. Work has become something you do by rote, because you have to. When your nose sticks too close to the grindstone, your very soul gets a grinding.

Take a step back. Look at the bigger picture. Work—your work—has a purpose in the larger scheme of things. Your work impacts other people. When you recognize and appreciate how your work allows you to matter in the world, you will see it with new eyes. Work ceases to be a daily slog and becomes a source of pride, accomplishment, and joy.

For example, you're not just an engineer who designs commercial air conditioning and heating systems. When you step back and take the larger view, you realize that you're making environments comfortable and healthy for people who work in the buildings with the systems you design. Your work contributes to the overall well-being of others, helping them be more effective and happier.

As a homemaker, you're not just cleaning the house, making meals, and picking up after the kids, you're contributing to your family's health and happiness. You're also contributing to the overall health and happiness of your community and your nation, since healthy and happy individuals make for a more viable society. Your work gives you this opportunity. When you look at it this way, you understand your work from a larger, more meaningful perspective from which you can draw pride and a deep sense of self-worth.

If you're a bookkeeper or an accountant, your purpose is to help individuals or companies keep their financial affairs in order so they can budget and spend wisely, which greatly minimizes their stress and contributes to their success and well-being.

Any work can be appreciated in this way: from running a mom-and-pop business to manual labor, from fundraising to waiting tables, from recording a song to inputting data. It doesn't matter what you do, your work has a purpose in the larger scheme of life.

When you look at your work as a part of the big picture, you recognize your value, your contribution to the whole of life, to our world. As you become aware of your purpose, you focus on a common intention with your co-workers, bosses, and customers, and your work acquires an ease or flow.

With a sense of purpose, work ceases to be drudgery and instead supports and enhances your life. Work brings you joy, and, in the process, brings joy to others.

So get your nose off that grindstone and enjoy the song your soul will sing!

Life is just one grand sweet song, so start the music.
—Anonymous

Making Dreams Come True

You have a dream in mind—something you want for you or your family—a home more suited to your needs, doing something meaningful for the world, a project you long to make happen, or a vacation longer than a week. Too often what stops you is the plaintive cry, "If only I had the money!" And you let your dream fade because you think the lack of money makes it unattainable. How sad! And how unnecessary.

You see, money is but one resource, and it's not always the most useful one.

Other resources, such as information and imagination, are often more powerful than money because with them you can obtain access to a never-ending wealth of solutions to a multitude of problems and challenges, including how to find the money!

People who are able to make their dreams come true are uncommonly good at recognizing and using the resources available to them. Their ability to do so arises from their belief that whatever they need is "out there" in some form and their willingness to search for resources creatively.

1) So how do you realize your dreams? Look for what's already "out there."

If developing technologies have brought on radical and often chaotic changes in how we work, play, and interact, they have also made abundant resources available to a degree never before enjoyed by the average person. The Internet alone has made us aware of the vast array of resources available to everyone on the planet who has access to a computer. Your local library has tremendous resources buried within its references and other sources, many of which are accessible online.

In addition to all that the Internet makes available to us, books, libraries, newspapers, magazines, television, radio, and films are excellent resources as well. One of my personal favorites is that wonderful, seemingly endless source of valuable information: the reference librarian. The information a reference librarian has to offer is limited only by the number of well-targeted questions you can come up with.

2) Use what's "out there" imaginatively.

Those able to achieve their goals are uncannily good at using an undervalued yet

tremendously powerful resource: their imagination. "My imagination!" you exclaim,
"Hogwash. I need a steady job, plain and
simple."

"And how do you think you're going to
get that steady job?" I ask.

"Look in the classifieds," you reply, being
the down-to-earth person that you are.

"Where else in the paper do you look for
jobs?"

"I don't." You answer my question slow-
ly, doing your best to be patient with my
obvious lack of common sense. "The classifieds are where they announce job openings."

"Right. And what about the information
in the rest of the paper?"
You frown, confused. "What about it?"

"Well, if you read the whole of the paper,
not just the classifieds, in order to see how
many different ideas you can find throughout to help you find or create a job that will
work for you, you'll be surprised at what you
find."

This is where your imagination kicks in.
You stop thinking of job hunting in the
paper as looking in the classifieds and start
treating the paper like a giant source of ideas
and information. You're not looking for a job
to pop out at you; you're looking for ideas on
how to get there. You notice low-cost train-
ing classes in various skills; free seminars
that introduce you to different ideas; com-

munity college classes and open houses for adults; support groups for people in transition; stories about how so-and-so turned a love of trinkets into a thriving mail-order business. "Hmm," you say, "I never thought about it that way."

Most people don't. The neat thing about the imagination is that it can be used in as many ways as you can imagine (how's that for a mind bender!). If you use your imagination to help yourself use information, you will find many ways to make your dreams come true. Money will then be but one dream-creating tool in the service of your incredible imagination.

Genius is the ability to put into effect what is in your mind.
—F. Scott Fitzgerald

Fighting over Family Finances

You don't understand what's wrong: you consider your husband and yourself to be perfectly rational human beings, yet every time you sit down to discuss the family finances, you get into a fight.

You want to save for medical emergencies, for the kid's education, for a new place to live, for retirement, to fix your on-again, off-again furnace—heck, you want to make sure your bases are covered before you go off and spend what little extra you have. Your husband wants to spend: the latest computer gizmo ("it's for work!"), a new unpronounceable something for the car, tickets to the game for all the guys. Any discussion of "Where did the money go?" ends up with, "You spent that much for what?"

With that, your husband gets defensive and accuses you of being a tightwad and no fun. You accuse him of not caring about you and the kids. Within minutes, you've gone from a reasonable conversation to screaming at each other to finally stomping off in hurt silence.

But since you love each other, you kiss and make up, and all is well until the next family finances meeting, when the same darn issues come up in the same way. And here you go fighting again in the same darn way. Is there any way to get off this highly unpleasant merry-go-round? Yes, indeed, but it's going to take a different approach.

1) Acknowledge your differences.

You can't fix what you won't acknowledge. There is no one way to deal with money. Certainly "savers" often feel more righteous than "spenders," but it's important to realize that both are essential to a healthy financial situation. Life is no fun if you're not spending some of that hard-won cash, just as life is no fun if there's nothing left for emergencies or long-term expenditures.

Sit down with your husband and write down what each of you wants to use your money for. Prioritize the items on your individual lists. Then, without judgement or criticism, exchange lists.

2) Accept your differences.

Look over your spouse's list without screaming. If you don't understand why he listed a certain desire, ask him in a neutral voice to talk to you about it. Don't argue with him, just listen.

192 — Dr. Noelle C. Nelson

3) Decide you can have it all.

This may sound impossible, yet if you decide you can both have what you want, then you can start working together to achieve it. Up until now, you've been pulling at each other, trying to get what you believe is the best use of your money, but in so doing, you've been tearing each other apart. Once you decide both your lists are valid, you can work together.

4) Set goals.

Decide which item you want to start with. Toss a coin if you don't know which one would be best. Establish a strategy for achieving your goals together. Think of yourselves as business partners working to make the business part of your marriage a success.

With that, you can have the fun of achieving your money goals. Your monthly finance meetings can be about checking your progress, regrouping as necessary, working on new strategies, and so on.

Lo and behold, now your finance sessions can bring you together rather than tear you apart.

Knowing is not enough; we must apply. Willing is not enough; we must do.

—Johann Wolfgang von Goethe

Bills, Bills, Bills!

Bills, bills, bills! That's all you see. And here it is, tax season, which for some lucky people might mean a refund, but for you, all it means is worry. You're a perfect bear at home: all you do is stomp around and grumble. Or that's what you're doing when you're not completely depressed staring at the pile of bills. All you can think about is how you never have enough money or can never afford what you want or why everything is so expensive. You're tired of hearing yourself complain. Heck, even the family dog is tired of hearing you complain, but what are you supposed to do? It's true!

Well, it may be true, but it's only part of the truth. The whole truth is that money can flow into your pockets just as it flows out. You are so focused on the "money flowing out" portion of the equation that you are virtually blind to the money flowing in.

Perception is a very strange thing. We tend to perceive what we are focused on, what we are interested in. Of all the information we are bombarded with in any given day, you only actually let in the information that is of interest to you. If you love cars, you notice where all the auto shops are in town, you spot that new sports car zipping along, you pay attention to the car commercials. If shoes are "it" for you, a hundred car ads could be in front of your nose and all you'd notice is the one shoe commercial buried in the midst of them.

So it is with money. Money is just as capable as flowing to you as away from you. It's a matter of focus. Instead of gluing your attention to the dollars going out, start noticing and valuing the dollars coming in! Deliberately turn your focus to noticing the many opportunities there are to make or save money and you will begin to perceive a whole host of ways to increase the abundance in your life.

Take notice when the telephone companies vie for your business, and shop for a less expensive phone plan. Introduce your family to the joys of hiking or making a scrapbook together rather than spending the day at the mall. Make yard sales and thrift shops a journey of discovery. Recognize that you can barter your services for some of what you need. In these ways, you will become open to more and more sources of abundance.

Now, notice I didn't say *dollars*, but rather used the word *abundance*. This is because if you are strictly looking for actual money (i.e. an increase in the number of dollars in your wallet), you are likely to miss the many ways in which you can become "richer" without the direct involvement of dollars. For example, if a friend invites you to lunch, you just became "richer" by one lunch. If they're handing out free preview movie passes at the supermarket, you just became "richer" by a pair of movie tickets. When you can barter your ability to tutor the neighbor's child in exchange for their babysitting for you, you just became "richer" by two babysitting sessions.

As you pay more attention to increasing the inflow of abundance rather than bemoaning the necessary outflow, your anxiety will decrease. You'll feel more in charge of your life and less like you're out there swinging in the wind at the mercy of all and sundry. You will recognize that you have a lot more control over your finances than you realized. Your mood will improve and your general enthusiasm for life will grow.

The more you start thinking in terms of increasing the flow of good things in your life, the more you'll perceive the opportunities to make that happen. It's all a matter of focus and perspective.

Reflect upon your blessings, of which every man has plenty, not on your past misfortunes, of which all men have some.
—Charles Dickens

Mixing Friends and Money

You're a good-humored, laid-back kind of person, so you don't "keep score" or pay too much attention to who's paying for what when you're out with your friends. But lately you can't help but notice—with one friend in particular—that you're always the one footing the bill. You mention it to him, and he apologizes. Your friend says he's going through a rough patch financially at the moment, and if you'd rather just not get together for a while, he'll understand. Well, you don't want that, and you certainly don't want to seem stingy. After all, who hasn't been through a rough patch?

You spring for your next few outings, no problem. Which would have been fine, except last night he started going on about this whoop-dee-do new computer he just bought. That stings, so you say, "I thought you were broke."

"It's for work, for crying out loud—how can you be so petty?" he shoots back. You wonder, "Am I being petty?"

Or maybe you're not so laid-back—you have a family or obligations, and you're on a budget. You're careful with your dollars, you plan what you can spend where, and an outing is a big deal to you. One of your other friends is always short almost every single time you go out. It's not much—$5 here, $7 there—but it adds up over time. You'd like to call her on it, but she always has a good excuse: "Oh, the ATM wasn't working, and this is all the cash I have on me"; or, "I didn't want to be late for us, I know how you hate it when people are late"; or, "I'll pay you back next time" (which she usually forgets to do). You feel resentful, but how can you get upset over $5 or $7 or even $10? Aren't friendships supposed to be about caring and sharing? You feel guilty for feeling resentful. How can you say anything? It seems too darn petty.

Sharing your feelings is never petty. Being willing and able to share your feelings is one of the most important elements of a friendship. If you're uncomfortable with how money is being handled in your friendship, whether it's your picking up the tab more often than feels good to you or picking up the slack for a friend who's always short, talk with your friend about your feelings.

Say, for example, "I'm feeling uncomfortable with being responsible for all our outing expenses. If you're still financially strapped, how about we come up with some things to do together that won't cost any money?" There are always things to do that are free of charge or close to it: you can take walks together, sit over a cup of coffee, visit art galleries, or go root for your local high-school athletes. Or, for your friend who relies too heavily on you to make up the difference, say, "I'm feeling uncomfortable with spending more than I've budgeted. My finances just can't handle it. What can we do so that I stay within my budget and you're okay with your share of the bill?"

If your friend doesn't want to hear about it, then your feelings aren't being respected. There is no "right" or "wrong" about who picks up the tab, but there is what's comfortable for each of you and what isn't. If your friend isn't willing to genuinely discuss the matter, it's not a good sign.

Whether it be a friendship or a marriage, any relationship in which the people involved can't discuss their feelings together isn't going to have much depth to it. If your friend listens to you, apologizes, but doesn't change their behavior, well, once again, your friendship may not be all that you thought it was. If, however, your friend says, "Gosh, I'm sorry, I didn't realize you were that uncomfortable. Sure, let's meet for coffee over at that new art gallery," or, "It's a bad habit, my never checking my wallet ahead of time. I'll pay more attention next time," and follows through, why then you have a true friend.

What a joy!

Emotion is not something shameful, subordinate, second-rate; it is a supremely valid phase of humanity at its noblest and most mature.

—Joseph Loth Liebman

Afterword

Appreciation is only meaningful when put into practice. Each of the chapters in this book has introduced ways to practice appreciation. Using the guidance provided throughout as a basis to start genuinely valuing yourself, those in your life, and the world we live in, you'll come almost immediately to realize the true power of appreciation. For example, you'll find that just by saying one appreciative thing a day to your spouse, your child, or your co-worker, your relationships will become more gratifying, more pleasurable, and will ultimately bring you greater happiness and enrichment.

Unlike gratitude or positive thinking, appreciation consists in actively looking for something of value in whatever you encounter. Like attracts like, and as you actively seek to value whatever is in your life right here, right now, you will in turn attract more things to value. Your very being becomes a vibratory match to that which you value, that which you appreciate, which is itself inevitably drawn to you energetically. Since all things exist first as energy before they can become matter, you are deliberately creating what you want in your life through the power and positive energy of appreciation.

The benefits are numerous. Science has repeatedly shown that the simple act of appreciating smoothes your heart rhythms so that your heart—and thus all the other systems it regulates—can function at their best. Thinking and feeling appreciation also supports greater blood flow to your brain, which makes it possible for your brain to function at its fullest capacity. You'll enjoy not only greater physical well-being, but also the possibility of increased health longevity. Centenarians have been shown to have one trait in common: appreciation of the stuff of everyday life.

In addition to the health benefits, appreciation helps to build self-esteem and self-confidence and works to counter depression. It is almost impossible to be depressed, angry, fearful, or anxious when you are vigorously appreciating! Relationships also benefit tremendously, be they relationships at home, at work, or in love. As relationships become stronger, more wholesome, and more expansive, so too will your success at work, at home, and in love. Genuine appreciation has only upsides; it is a marvelous foundation for so many of the other things we value, such as love, creativity, energy, well-being, and success.

Appreciation takes courage, for it isn't always easy to find the value in something. Difficult people and challenging situations exist in all of our lives. Nonetheless, doing your best to appreciate in all circumstances will ensure greater happiness and success than would otherwise be possible.

You deserve the very best that life has to offer. May this book help you to appreciate as much and as often as you can the love, joy, success, and abundance that is yours—for the appreciating!

INDEX

READING GROUP GUIDE

Who are the key characters in each chapter?

Do you empathize with any of the characters? Are the characters or their circumstances familiar to you? If so, how? What has been your own experience of such situations?

What do the characters do in each chapter?

Do the characters react as you would in a similar situation? Do you find their actions understandable? How so?

Is the advice or insight given in each chapter helpful?

How does the advice or insight given help the characters? Would you follow such recommendations? What advice has been given to you in similar circumstances? How does it compare to the advice and insight offered here?

What is the book about?

Does the book have a central theme? If so, what? Does it have multiple themes? If so, can you identify them?

What do you know about the author?

Is the book autobiographical? Do you feel that the author has brought her own experience to the book? Have you read any other books by the author? If so, are they similar in style or content? Does the author show any growth or change in her approach to this book?

How did the book affect you?

Do you feel changed in any way from reading the book? Did it give you insights or tools for personal growth you didn't have before? How might you use the insights or advice in the future? Did reading the book help you better understand a situation in your own life or in that of a friend?

What did you like or dislike?

Did you like the book? What did you like or dislike most? Did you have any expectations of the book? If so, did it live up to them? Had you read any reviews before reading it? If so, do you find yourself agreeing with the reviews? Would you give the book as a gift? Who would you give it to? Would you read it again?